The Challenge of Jesus

James Nelson and Juliana McNeice

Colourpoint Educational

ISBN 0 898392 50 1

8 7 6 5 4

Layout and design: Colourpoint Books
Cover design: Barry Craig for Colourpoint
Printed by: W & G Baird Ltd

Colourpoint Books
Colourpoint House
Jubilee Business Park
21 Jubilee Road
NEWTOWNARDS
Co Down
BT23 4YH

Tel: 028 9182 0505
Fax: 028 9182 1900
E-mail: info@colourpoint.co.uk

The Authors

James Nelson has been a Head of RE and is now a lecturer in Religious Studies in Stranmillis University College, Belfast.

Juliana McNeice is Head of Religious Studies in Rainey Endowed School, Magherafelt, Co Londonderry. She has a BEd in Religious Studies.

Picture credits
Hutchison Picture Library 5, 13, 14, 19, 22, 24, 46, 66
Ronald Grant Archive 50
Kobal Collection 16, 30, 63, 67
e.t. archive/DACS 65
Topham Picturepoint 33, 41, 53, 69
Tony Stone Images 20, 35, 44, 64
Norman Johnston 17, 40
James Nelson 11

We are indebted to Sam Smith of the Leprosy Mission for kindly supplying the pictures on page 59.

Grateful thanks also to Gary Hewitt of the National Trust for Northern Ireland for the pictures on page 32.

PLM

Contents

This book is dedicated to the memory of Cyril McNeice (1927-1999)

Introduction

The primary intention of this book is to provide a resource for Religious Studies which directly meets the needs of the "Challenge of Jesus" section of the Northern Ireland Core Syllabus at Key Stage 4. It is hoped that it lends itself to creative and interactive classroom practice and that a use may also be found for it in non-school contexts such as youth groups and church organisations.

Throughout we have tried to reflect on the material's relevance for young people and Christians today. In doing so we have used a variety of local and contemporary sources. In particular we are grateful for the help of:
- Sam Smith of the Leprosy Mission
- Michael Hanly and Barbara Hughes of the Volunteer Missionary Movement

Once again we would like to thank Colourpoint for their consistent professionalism and ability to transform black and white copy into vibrant and colourful text.

Finally, a special thanks to Sarah and Martin for their patience and unconditional support.

James Nelson and **Juliana McNeice**, June 1999

All Biblical references are taken from *The Good News Bible* unless stated otherwise

The following symbols are used throughout the book to guide the reader in finding particular references:

Discussion

Activity

Questions

Israel, looking towards the Red Sea

Palestine at the time of Jesus

Imagine that, in 1000 years time, someone were to look back and try to find out about your life. They might find out about where you were born, your family, what school you went to, what you did in your spare time and who your friends were, but they would only really understand you if they knew more about the culture of the time and the type of society you lived in.

It is important for us then, when looking back 2000 years to study the life of Jesus, to find out as much as possible about the place and time in which he lived. Let us begin by exploring the geographical, political, social and religious background of Palestine at the time of Jesus.

Geographical Context

The area in which Jesus lived out his life was known as **Palestine**. Today the modern countries of Israel and Palestine occupy this land. It is an extremely important region to three of the world's main religions (Judaism, Islam and Christianity) for whom it has deep, sacred significance. If you look at the map on page 6 you can see it also holds a central geographical position forming a bridge between the continents of Europe, Asia and Africa.

Jerusalem, the capital of Palestine, was already an ancient city at the time of Jesus and had a population of about 50,000 people. The narrow streets were often overcrowded with traders and travellers as it was part of the main trade corridor running between Asia and Africa. Also at festival time many people went to visit Jerusalem to carry out their religious duties. Of course many things about Jerusalem have changed but it is still as crowded with tourists and religious believers today.

One other thing about this region which has remained the same is its climate. The temperatures of this area mean that it is a land of contrasts – there are large areas of desert, yet the mountains also cause rain and areas near the main rivers are fertile and green.

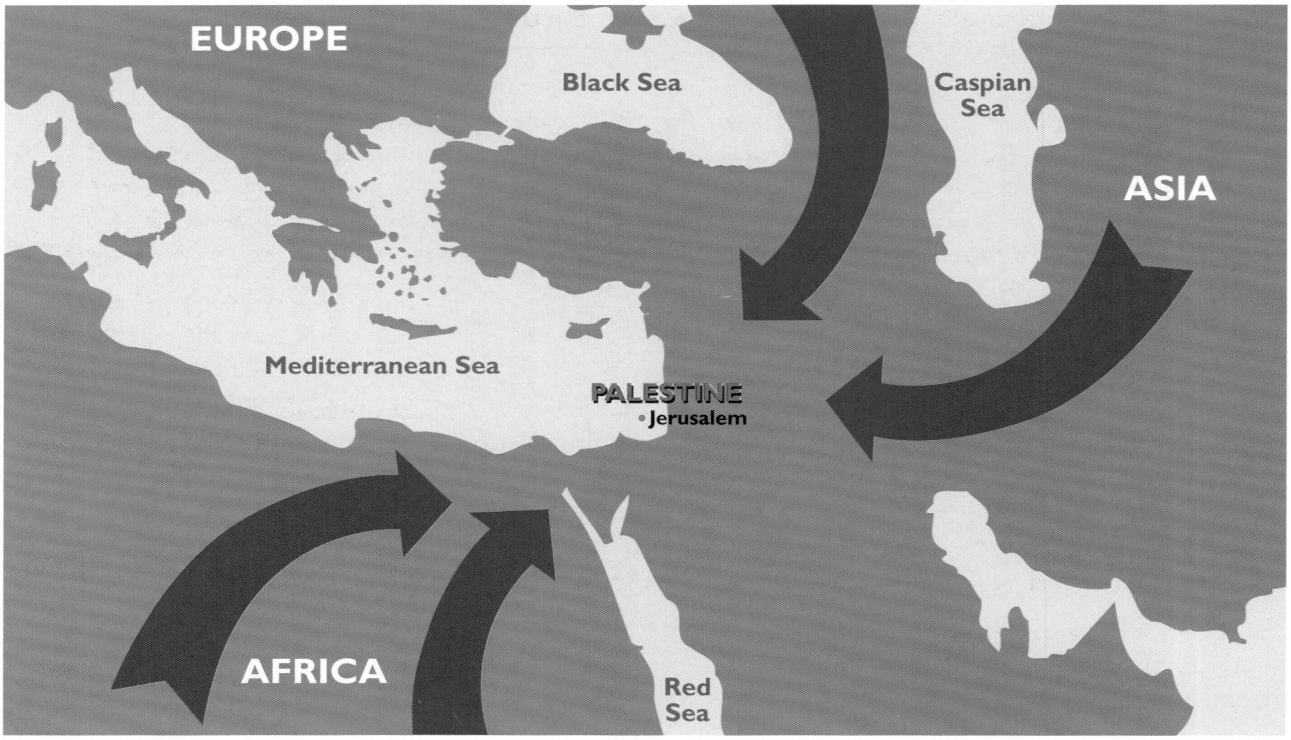

Palestine – the bridge between Europe, Asia and Africa.

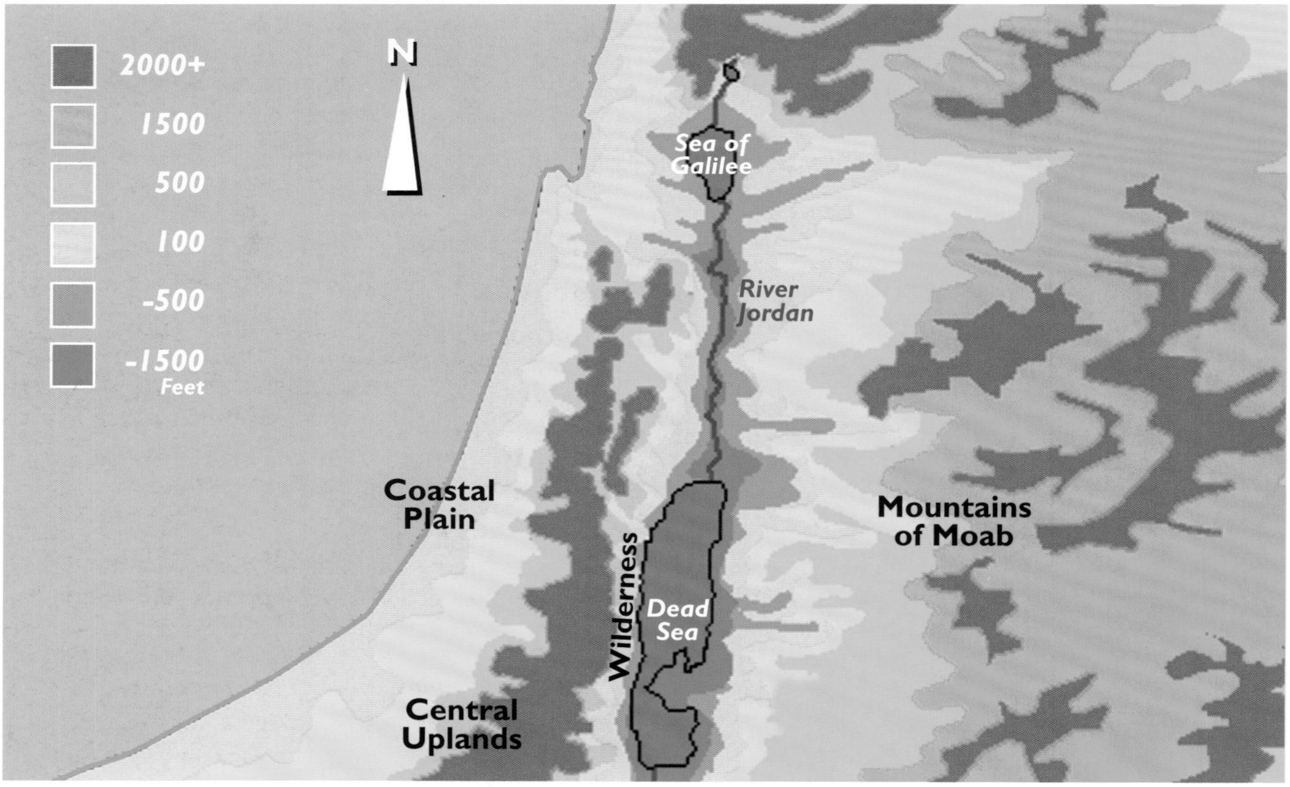

Palestine – a land of contrasts.

Ben is an Israeli tour-guide who describes here what the climate of Israel is like:

Israel's climate ranges from temperate to tropical. There are 2 main seasons – a rainy winter period from November to May and a dry summer season for the other 6 months. Rainfall is heavy in the north and centre of the country with almost nothing in the south. The landscape is also extremely varied - from the sandy beaches of the Mediterranean coast to the rolling hills of Samaria and Judaea and the bare, craggy peaks, craters and plateaus of the desert. We have something for everyone in Israel and I recommend you make a visit!

The map on page 6 shows the variety of land-types across this region. The main features are the Coastal Plain, the Central Uplands, the Wilderness of Judaea, the Sea of Galilee, the River Jordan and the Dead Sea.

The Coastal Plain

This is a flat area which runs along the majority of the Palestinian coast line, from Sidon in the north to Gaza in the south. It is composed of a sandy shoreline and occasional cliffs which drop dramatically to the sea.

The Central Uplands

These hills thread their way through the length of Palestine and include the Uplands of Galilee, the Uplands of Samaria and the Uplands of Judaea.

The Wilderness of Judaea

To the east of the Uplands of Judaea lies the Wilderness of Judaea. This desolate area is mentioned in the Bible as a place where John the Baptist spent much time and where Jesus was tempted.

The River Jordan

The Jordan river runs from the Uplands of Galilee into the Sea of Galilee, then through the Rift Valley and into the Dead Sea. While it swells in winter during the rainy season, it is usually quite narrow and shallow.

The Sea of Galilee

The northern area, around Galilee, is where Jesus would have spent much of his life. The Sea of Galilee is really a lake but is 13 miles long and 7 miles wide so it looks more like a sea. It is also called Lake Gennesaret in Luke's Gospel.

The Dead Sea

The Dead Sea, also known as the Salt Sea, is almost 400 metres below sea-level, which makes it the lowest point on earth. Due to the intense temperatures at the sea, water evaporates extremely rapidly and leaves very high levels of salt deposits. As a result fish cannot survive in it, but it also means that a human cannot sink in it!

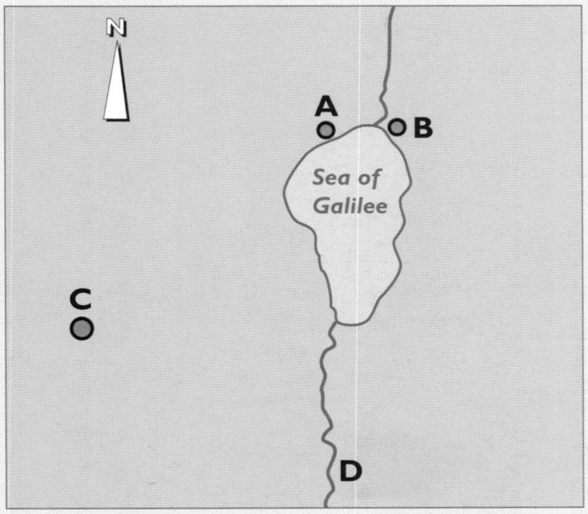

Activity

a) Look up the following references to find out the names of the places on the map.

A = Matthew 4:13
B = Luke 9:10
C = Matthew 2:23
D = Matthew 3:5-6

b) Various events in Jesus' life took place in and around Galilee. Look up the following references and write a sentence on each event.

(i) Luke 2:39
(ii) Matthew 8:24, 26, 27
(iii) Luke 8:40-42
(iv) Matthew 14:25-26
(v) Matthew 28:7,10,16

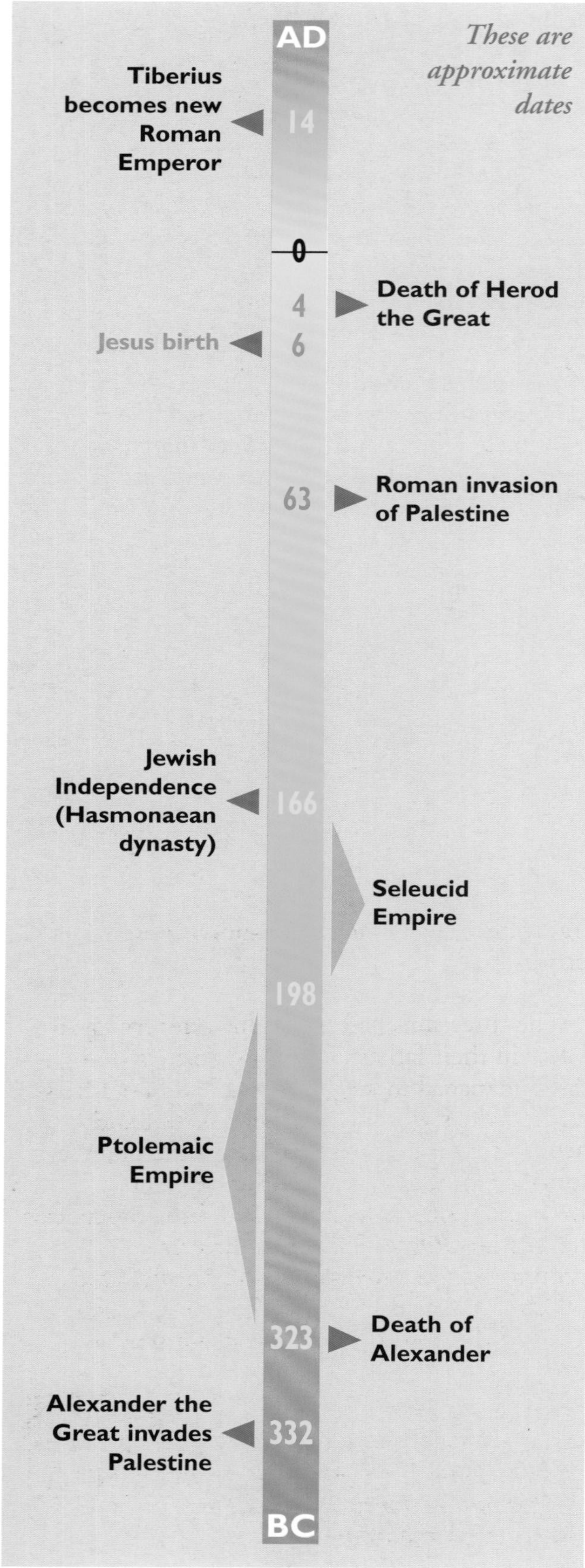

Historical Context

Because of its central geographical position in the ancient world Palestine was fought over many times as governments and armies valued its strong strategic position. The timeline on the left shows the main leaders who controlled this small strip of land in the centuries leading up to the birth of Jesus.

Alexander the Great, founder of the Greek Empire, took over Palestine in 332 BC. When Alexander died, his lands were divided among several generals who each established their own dynasties. Two of these dynasties, those of **Ptolemy** and **Seleucus**, controlled Palestine at different times from 323 BC to 166 BC.

Many Jews were unhappy living under the control of Greek rulers. Eventually, in 168 BC, a revolt to overthrow the Seleucids was led by **Judas Maccabeus** and his brothers. After a long, hard struggle they managed to achieve independence and their family name, **Hasmonean**, was given to the new dynasty. This period of Jewish self-rule did not last long and in 63 BC they were soon under the control of another foreign power – the **Romans**.

Activity

Imagine you are a tour guide in first century Palestine. Design a colourful, friendly brochure which introduces people to the main tourist attractions.

Questions

1. ***Why was Palestine considered to be an important geographical location?***
2. ***What was the Sea of Galilee also known as?***
3. ***Where is the lowest point on earth?***
4. ***Name an important event in Jesus' life which happened in the wilderness of Judaea.***

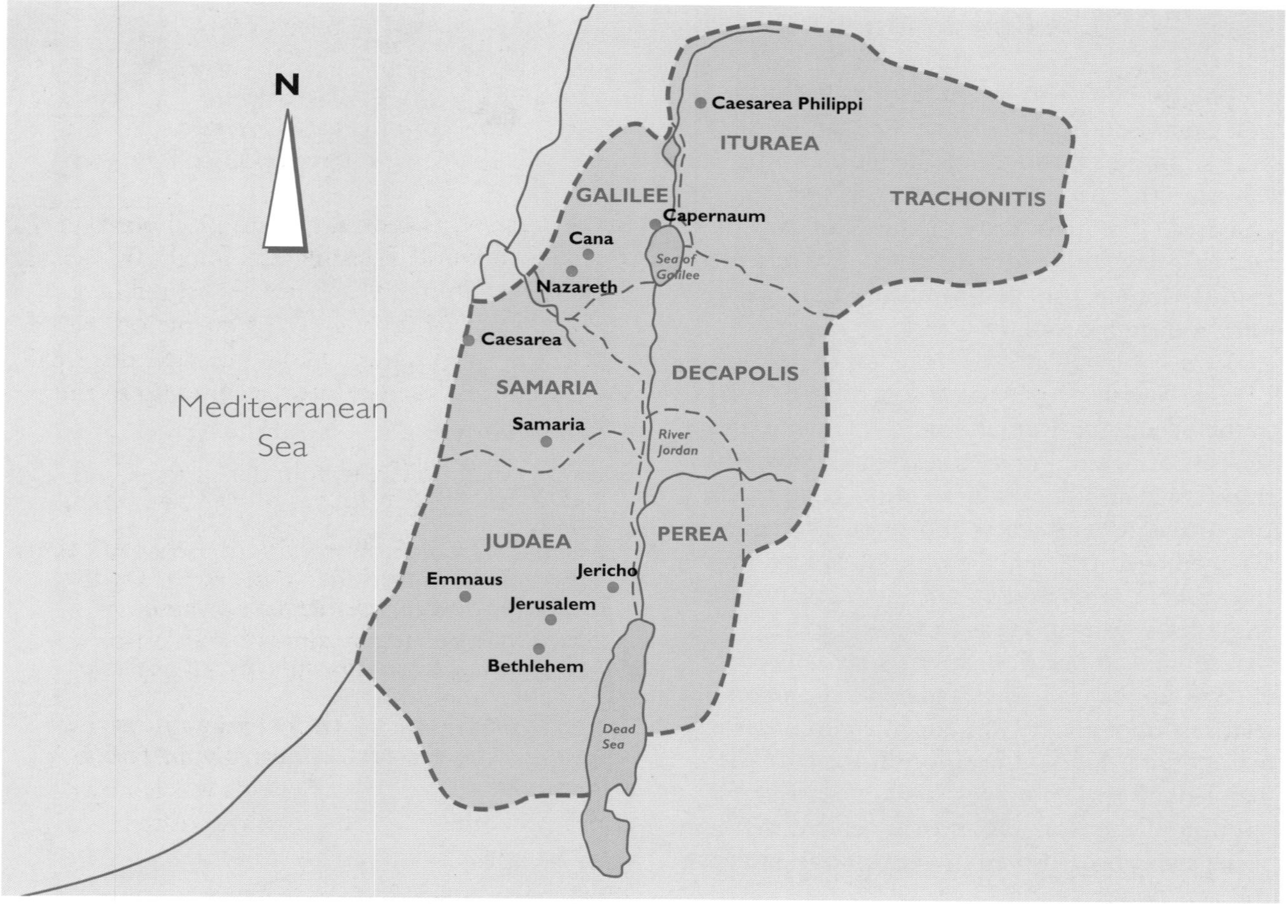

Palestine at the time of Jesus.

Political background

In 31 BC the Roman Empire was established under the control of **Caesar Augustus**. When Jesus was born, Palestine was governed by **Herod the Great** (37-4 BC). Herod had the title 'King of the Jews' and could trace his Jewish roots back to Judas Maccabeus, but he was only half-Jewish and many Jewish people found him to be an unacceptable ruler because he did as he was told by the Romans. So he was considered a 'puppet-King' and not a true ruler of the Jewish people. Herod could be a ruthless man and ordered the murder of several of his wives and sons. When he died in 4 BC he left his kingdom to be divided between three of his favourite sons: **Herod Antipas** who took charge of Galilee and Perea; **Herod Archelaus** who took charge of Judaea and Samaria; and **Philip the Tetrarch** who took charge of Iturea and Trachonitis. The map above shows these territories.

The three sons had mixed fortunes trying to follow in their father's footsteps. Antipas and Philip managed to keep a steady hand on affairs but Archelaus was such a cruel, corrupt and incompetent leader that he was deposed by the Romans and replaced by a **procurator** (a government official). In AD 26-36 the procurator was **Pontius Pilate**. Pilate was directly accountable to Rome and was responsible for collecting taxes and keeping the peace, which included the power to pass the death sentence.

Activity

Copy the timeline into your notes and add in the extra dates and events mentioned above.

The Roman army

The Roman army was a highly-disciplined, well-organised fighting force. Roman soldiers were stationed throughout the land and in Palestine the army headquarters was at Caesarea. The main duty of the army was to maintain law and order, to crush any rebellions against Roman rule and to ensure that taxes were collected properly.

The Jewish people reacted in different ways to the occupying Roman force. A few saw the benefits of belonging to an extremely powerful empire which had money to build good roads, amphitheatres and water and sewage systems. They enjoyed the benefits of good law and order, an excellent army and an advanced legal system. Some Jews went so far as to work for the government in positions such as tax-collectors; the **Sadducees** (religious leaders), kept a good relationship with the Roman rulers in order to maintain a privileged position in society. The majority of Jews, however, had a negative opinion of the Romans and felt bullied by them. Some even showed their anger through violence and acts of aggression.

Tax Collectors

Palestine was divided into tax districts and the taxes were collected by local people who were employed by the Romans. Jews who worked for the Romans were despised for two main reasons:

- They worked for the Roman government. The Jews considered the Romans to be an occupying force in their land and therefore the tax collectors were regarded as traitors.
- It was a common practice for tax collectors to charge people more than was required by the Romans, so they could make a large profit themselves. The Jews therefore considered them to be cheats and liars.

Matthew, one of Jesus' disciples, had been a tax collector (Matthew 9:9-12) and Zacchaeus, a chief tax-collector, became a follower of Jesus (Luke 19:1-10).

Activity

Copy the map of Palestine into your notes and place the names of Herod's sons in the regions they ruled.

Questions

1 What Emperors ruled the Roman Empire during Jesus' lifetime?
2 a) Who ruled Palestine at the time of Jesus' birth?
b) What was King Herod the Great's other title?
c) Why could this be considered a misleading title?
3 Name Herod the Great's sons who took over the rule of Palestine.
4 What duties did the Roman army have throughout the Empire?
5 a) What opinion did the majority of Jews have of the Romans?
b) Explain why you think this was the case.
6 Why were the tax-collectors not popular people?

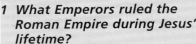

Social & Religious Background

The religious tradition of Jesus' parents, Mary and Joseph, was Judaism. This meant that Jesus was a descendant of Abraham, the father of the Jewish nation. Abraham had made a **covenant** (agreement) with God that he would worship and obey him if God blessed him and made his family into a great nation. Abraham's descendants sometimes struggled to keep their part of the agreement, but they always returned to God (Yahweh) and their traditions survived.

The Temple

At first the Jews worshipped God in a movable temple which suited their nomadic lifestyle. It was a tent-like structure and was called the **Tabernacle**. (Exodus chapters 25-27 contain a detailed description of the Tabernacle.) When they became a settled community they

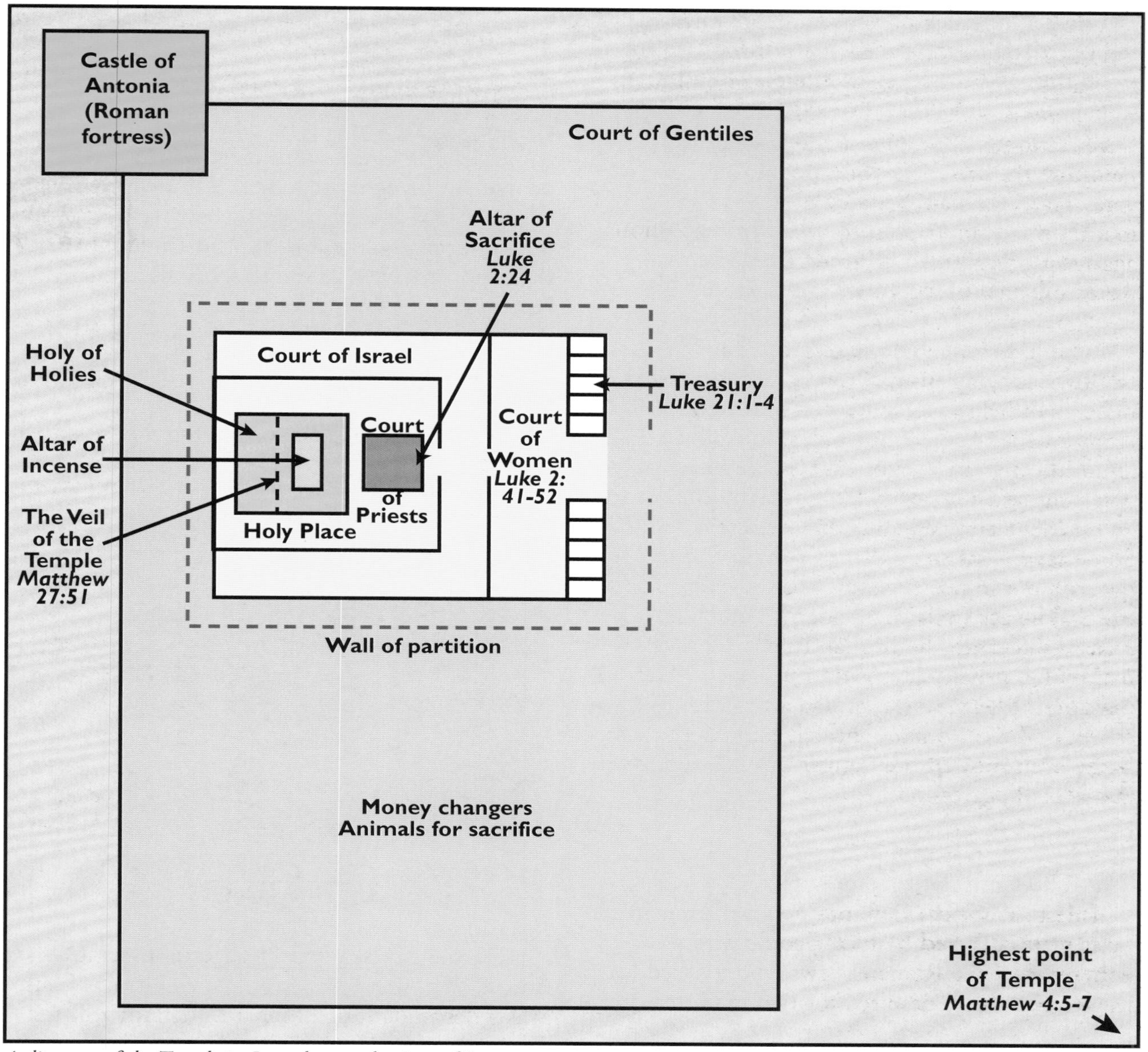

A diagram of the Temple in Jerusalem at the time of Jesus.

built a permanent **Temple** in Jerusalem for their worship. King Solomon was the first to build the Temple, but it was destroyed in time of war. By the time of Jesus a new Temple was being constructed in Jerusalem by Herod the Great. It was an impressive structure which took eighty years to complete. Sadly it was destroyed by the Romans only a few years later, in AD 70. All that remains of it now is the 'Western' or 'Wailing' Wall.

The Western, or 'Wailing', Wall in Jerusalem.

The Temple was spacious and contained the Temple markets, the courts for worship, a place of sacrifice and the Holy of Holies. The diagram on page 11 shows what it was like.

The Temple was divided into 5 main parts:

◆ **The Court of Gentiles**
This was the first courtyard inside the wall of the Temple and the only area where a Gentile (non-Jew) could enter. Here people changed money into coinage suitable for the Temple offering and bought animals for sacrifice. Coins had to be changed as Roman coins bearing Caesar's head were not acceptable, and sacrifices were bought here as they had already been checked for purity by the Temple inspectors.

◆ **The Court of Women**
Women were allowed to enter this court but could not go beyond it. The Temple treasury was kept here.

◆ **The Court of Israel**
Jewish men were allowed into this court which ran around three sides of the Holy Place. Jewish men and Priests came here to pray.

◆ **The Court of Priests**
Animal sacrifices took place at the Altar in this court and only Priests could enter here.

◆ **The Holy Place**
This building was divided into two by a curtain called 'The Veil'. Priests could enter the Holy Place to burn incense, but only once a year on the day of Atonement would the High Priest go beyond the veil into the Holy of Holies, where the Ark of the Covenant, containing the Ten Commandments, was kept.

Activity

Look up the Bible references listed on the diagram on page 11 to see where parts of the Temple are mentioned in the Gospels.

Synagogue

The Jews had only one Temple, but for those who did not live in Jerusalem there were **synagogues** to worship in. The word 'synagogue' comes from a Greek word meaning 'gathering of people' or 'bringing together'. All towns with at least ten Jewish men had a synagogue – it was a house of prayer and a place of instruction where the scriptures were read and sermons preached, but no sacrifices could be made.

Some Romans and Greeks also attended Synagogue worship. These people were attracted to Judaism's belief in one God, its strong morality, and its ancient traditions. They were known as **god-fearers** and were allowed to attend the synagogue services and hear the teaching there.

Plan of a synagogue

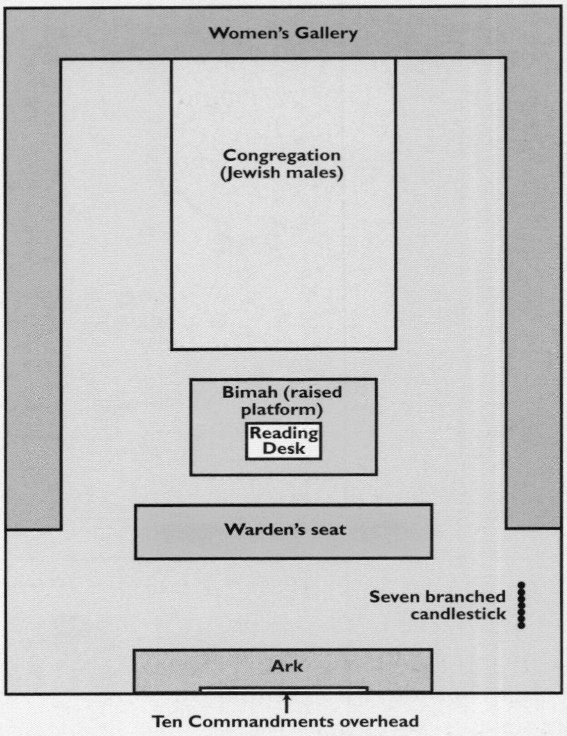

Activity

The following references show the importance of the synagogue in 1st century Palestine. Make a note about each story.

(a) Matthew 13:53-58 ***(b) Luke 4:38-39***
(c) Luke 4:44 ***(d) Luke 7:1-5***
(e) Luke 8:41-42 ***(f) Luke 13:10-17***

Religious groups

Just as there are many different groups within the Christian Church today, so there were various religious parties within Judaism.

1. The Pharisees

These were the religious leaders who had most contact with ordinary people. They lived by a strict set of rules and guidelines called the Oral Law. Jesus often criticised their rule-keeping in the Gospels as he said they kept religious laws but didn't have genuine faith or love in their hearts. Many Pharisees became enemies of Jesus because they believed his teaching threatened their Law.

The Pharisees believed that God could intervene in everyday life and that a Messiah would come from God to deliver them from their hardships, leading them into an era of religious and political good fortune. They also believed in life after death and bodily resurrection.

2. The Sadducees

These were the priestly, upper class of the religious leaders. They enjoyed a privileged life which was possible because of their good relationship with the Romans. The Sadducees did not believe in the idea of a Messiah and they did not accept the Oral Law or the idea of a bodily resurrection after death. The Sadducees joined with the Pharisees against Jesus because he criticised them and they saw him as a threat to their relationship with the Romans.

3. The High Priest

The High Priest was the religious leader of the Jews. He was the only person allowed to enter The Holy of Holies, which was where God's presence resided on earth. The High Priest was also in charge of the Sanhedrin, the highest Jewish Council. Caiaphas was the High Priest at the time of Jesus.

4. The Essenes

This group tried to lead lives of religious purity and withdrew from normal, everyday life. They lived in communities dedicated to worshipping and serving God. They farmed their land and shared all their possessions. They were celibate and, as well as praying and discussing religious matters together, they would have helped the sick and elderly. One Essene community may have been at Qumran, a site near the Dead Sea where famous scrolls (The Dead Sea Scrolls) were discovered in 1948.

The caves in which the Dead Sea Scrolls were found.

5. The Scribes

A scribe copied out the scriptures and had a sound grasp of written Law in the Old Testament. They are often referred to in the Gospels as the 'teachers of the Law'.

6. The Zealots

Simon, one of Jesus' disciples, was a Zealot (Luke 6:15). This group was passionate about the Jewish faith which included the belief that God had promised Abraham that the Jewish people would have a land of their own. The Zealots considered the Romans to be an occupying force in their land and they were prepared to fight against them in order to gain their political and religious independence. They refused to pay their taxes and on some occasions they attempted rebellions. The Romans did not tolerate this kind of dissent and on several occasions tried to wipe out this revolutionary group, but it took over 60 years to do so. The Zealots' last stand was in Masada, a fort on top of a mountain which the Romans could only reach by building a huge ramp. By the time they got there, however, the Zealots had all killed themselves – a final act of defiance against the Romans.

7. The Samaritans

Samaria lay between Galilee and Judaea. The people who lived there, the Samaritans, were a mixed race, only partly Jewish. They were descended from Jews who had intermarried with foreigners when the Assyrians invaded Israel in the eighth century BC.

The Samaritans worshipped the same God as the Jews and accepted part of their Law, but the Jews considered them to be inferior. Over time the Jews and Samaritans grew to hate each other.

This man is a modern Samaritan.

Activity

Copy and complete the following table:

Religious group	Place in society	Main beliefs

Discussion

a) Imagine you had to fill a "Millennium Box" containing items which say something about life at the beginning of the 21st century. The box would be buried under a sign which read "Not to be opened until 1 January 3000". What would you put in the box and why?

b) Imagine you found a box which had been buried in 1st century Palestine. What do you think you might find in it and what would it tell you about life two thousand years ago? (For example, you might find a Roman soldier's helmet or a coin from the Temple treasury.)

Questions

1 ***Explain why the Jews disliked the Samaritans.***
2 ***Name two religious groups who opposed Jesus and explain why they did so.***
3 ***a) Do you think the Zealots were right to use violence to defend what they believed?***
b) In your opinion is it ever right to use violence in the name of God or religion?

D	P	Z	D	K	Z	S	H	J	U	V	H	Z	X	C
S	T	O	L	A	E	Z	Q	F	G	P	T	F	J	D
B	Y	N	N	Y	C	S	R	G	G	D	U	A	H	E
C	I	N	S	T	Q	D	S	H	D	R	V	W	L	C
W	P	H	A	R	I	S	E	E	S	A	G	P	T	C
D	K	E	N	G	N	U	O	T	N	X	M	T	L	E
X	S	B	H	W	O	V	S	K	A	E	L	P	E	E
K	F	A	E	D	D	G	P	P	T	P	S	L	K	G
H	Y	I	D	E	D	M	U	N	I	G	I	X	U	Q
V	J	O	R	D	A	N	K	E	R	L	U	J	J	K
Z	D	Q	I	H	U	S	F	B	A	D	A	M	K	O
I	E	G	N	Y	U	C	B	G	M	T	O	T	C	A
F	W	W	F	L	D	M	E	L	A	S	U	R	E	J
F	F	H	M	M	P	A	L	E	S	T	I	N	E	N
C	X	P	S	N	L	T	K	V	S	R	B	D	J	H

Background to Palestine

There are 14 words (names, places or titles) in the word square.

You will have come across all of these words in this unit. When you discover the words, write a sentence about each to explain what they mean.

'Ben Hur, MGM, 1959

The Identity of Jesus

What did Jesus look like? Was he born like other people? Was he really the son of God? Was he the leader of a disorganised band of freedom fighters?

These are some of the questions people today ask about the identity of Jesus. In this unit we will try to investigate the question 'Who was Jesus?' through a study of relevant Biblical texts.

Birth of Jesus

The birth of a new baby is a very special time and causes much fuss and excitement. Christians celebrate new birth as a special gift from God and a sign of his power as Creator. Generally, there is a **naming** or **christening** ceremony and the baby is also given presents. Some of these customs and traditions were also associated with the birth of Jesus but, as we shall see, it was no ordinary birth.

The **birth narratives** (the Bible passages which tell the story of Christ's birth) are full of references to the importance of Jesus' birth. It is described as an **incarnation**, which means God coming to earth and taking on human form. Both Matthew and Luke try to explain this idea by pointing out all the signs which show that Jesus was not just another child but God's son and the **Messiah**, the person the Jews expected would come to establish God's rule on earth. Matthew, in particular, explains that Jesus' birth had been foretold by Old Testament prophets, such as Isaiah, which suggests he was the long-awaited Messiah. Luke suggests the same thing by saying Jesus will sit on 'the throne of his father David'. It was expected that the Messiah would be from King David's family line.

Jesus' birth foretold

Luke 1:26-56

Mary was told about Jesus' birth by an angel. Throughout the birth stories in Matthew and Luke there are frequent appearances by angels, miraculous happenings and dreams. On this occasion Mary was told that she would have a child. This passage is often referred to as **The Annunciation.** Luke reports that Mary was confused by the news and did not understand how she could be pregnant. However, Luke does not spend time explaining the details of this 'virgin birth'; it is more important to him to show us how Mary's child was special:

- He would sit on David's throne.
- He would be called the **Son of God** (see pages 26-27).

When Mary heard that she was to have a baby she was very happy and went to share the good news with her relative, Elizabeth. Elizabeth was pregnant with John the Baptist and she felt the baby move inside her when Mary arrived. She knew something special had happened. At that moment Mary sang a song of praise to God because she was so happy. This is often referred to as **The Magnificat.** If you look closely at Luke 1: 46-56 it can be divided into 4 parts:

1 Mary praises God and recognises her own unworthiness (v46-47).
2 She focuses on God's mightiness, holiness and mercy (v48-51).
3 She emphasises that God is not impressed by the rich or great people of the world but is primarily concerned with the poor and humble (v52-53).
4 Lastly, she looks back to how God has always worked through people in the past to bring his mercy and help to humans (v54-56).

Focus on Mary

Mary holds a very special place in the Christian faith as the mother of Jesus. This is highlighted in particular by the Roman Catholic Church which believe that Mary is blessed with some very special characteristics:

1 The title **Mother of God**

2 The **Immaculate Conception** – this means Mary herself was without sin and perfect:

The most Blessed Virgin Mary was, from the first moment of her conception ... preserved immune from all stain of original sin.

Pope Pius X, *Ineffabilis Deus*

3 A **Perpetual Virgin** – after giving birth to Jesus, Mary had no more children, but remained pure.

4 The **Assumption** – Mary did not die a normal, physical death:

When the course of her earthly life was finished, [she] was taken up body and soul into heavenly glory, and exalted by the Lord as Queen over all things, so that she might be the more fully conformed to her Son.

Pope Pius XII, *Munificentissimus Deus*

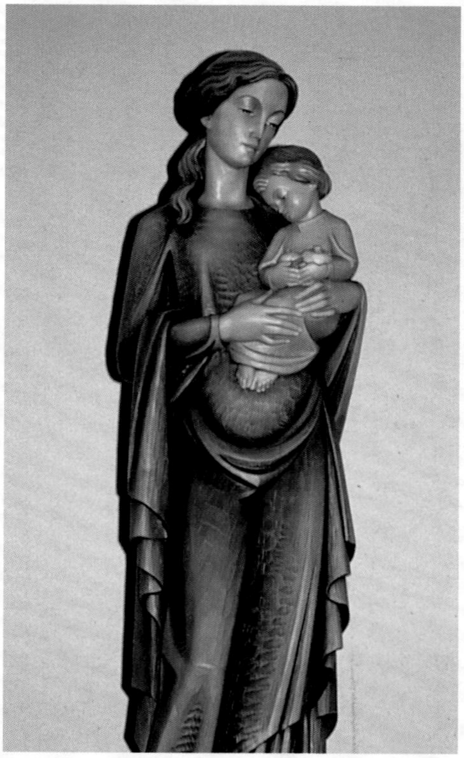

This statue of Mary and baby Jesus, often called a Madonna and Child, is in St Michael's Church, Enniskillen.

Jesus' birth

Matthew 1:18-24

Firstly, we learn that Mary and Joseph were not a married couple but were merely engaged. The discovery that they were going to have a child was something of a shock, particularly to Mary as she had no experience of a sexual relationship. Joseph must have been horrified and he made plans to separate from Mary as it seemed to him that she must have had an affair with another man; the Jewish law condemned such behaviour as punishable by death. However, Joseph was persuaded to change his mind through a dream where it was explained to him that Mary's child was conceived by the Holy Spirit. In this passage Matthew begins to draw to the reader's attention the importance and difference of this birth. He says:

- that the name 'Jesus' itself tells us something important about this child, because it means that he would save people from their sins;
- that he should be called **Immanuel** which means 'God with us'.

A virgin birth

In both of the passages above, it is made clear that Mary was a virgin when she conceived Jesus. This fulfilled a prediction in Isaiah 7:14 which stated:

"A virgin will become pregnant and have a son, and he will be called Immanuel."

Christians today are divided over whether this was a real miracle and an actual historical event or simply a story which symbolises the special and unique nature of Jesus.

Activity

In groups look at the following opinions. Which do you agree with most? Try to think of other reasons which explain your attitude to the virgin birth.

"The birth stories of Christ are just like the Creation stories of Genesis – neither contains scientific facts but both contain spiritual truths: God created the world; and Jesus was sent from God."

"God is all-powerful and capable of doing any miracles, therefore the virgin birth is a possibility."

"The Bible is a factual account, and if it says there was a virgin birth, then it can only mean there was an actual virgin birth."

"It cannot be proved that the virgin birth happened."

"Matthew and Luke wrote their stories many years after the actual birth of Jesus and they were looking back on the event, telling it as a legend rather than a factual account."

The shepherds

Luke 2:1-20

We are reminded in this passage that Jesus belonged to the family of David and was born in Bethlehem, the town of David. This was important for Luke as it was further proof that Jesus was the Messiah, because it was predicted in the Old Testament that the ruler over Israel would come out of Bethlehem (Micah 5:2).

According to Luke, when Jesus was born some of the first people to hear about it were shepherds in nearby fields. Being a shepherd was not considered a privileged position in society, so it would seem that the message about Christ was primarily for those considered insignificant or marginalised. At first the shepherds were very afraid but the angels assured them that the message was one of great news. An army of angels appeared singing praises to God (v14) which is now known as the **Gloria in Excelsis**. You may recognise this phrase from Christmas Carols.

Visitors from the east

Matthew 2:1-12

A large number of stories and traditions have grown up around these mysterious individuals from the east. It is widely assumed, for example, that three kings dressed in the finest clothes came to visit Jesus at the same time as the shepherds, but Matthew says nothing of the sort. He calls them **Magi, wise men**, not kings; he doesn't tell us how many there were; and they came to visit some weeks, if not months, after the shepherds, when Mary and Joseph had found accommodation in a house (v11).

The wise men have a symbolic role to play in this birth narrative. Coming from the east, they represent the **Gentile** (non-Jewish) world coming to worship this new King of the Jews. Their gifts are also highly symbolic of the type of person Jesus would be during his life.

- **Gold** is a precious metal and represents royalty. It emphasises Jesus' role as ruler over the Kingdom of God.
- **Frankincense** was a resin taken from a tree and burned for its smell during Temple worship. It represents Christ's Priestly role, as a link between God and his people.
- **Myrrh** was an oil used to anoint the dead. This represents Christ's humanity and death.

The wise men had tried to get Herod's help when they arrived in Jerusalem looking for the child. When Herod heard, he was insulted by the suggestion that there was another 'King of the Jews' and wanted to kill him. He wanted the help of the wise men in finding Jesus and pretended that he too wanted to worship the new baby.

Escape to Egypt

Matthew 2:13-23

More prophesies were fulfilled when Jesus was taken to Egypt for a time by Mary and Joseph, and Herod killed all two year olds and under in the area around Bethlehem (**the Slaughter of the Innocents**). This story sounds very similar to that of Moses in Egypt when the Pharaoh tried to kill all the Israelite children. It may be that Matthew is making another symbolic reference, this time to Jesus as a new Moses who would lead people to an even greater promised land. When Herod died in 4BC the family returned from Egypt, but not to Judaea. They were afraid of the new king, Archelaus, who was a cruel and sadistic ruler, so they moved on to Nazareth where Jesus spent the rest of his childhood.

Jesus is presented in the Temple

Luke 2:21-38

Luke is the only Gospel writer who gives us any details about the early childhood of Jesus. Firstly he tells us that, like all other Jewish boys, Jesus was circumcised and named after eight days. Because Jesus was the first-born boy of his family it also meant that he had to be consecrated in a special way. This involved offering a sacrifice at the Temple in Jerusalem to give thanks for the gift of a son.

While in the Temple Jesus met the elderly **Simeon** and **Anna**. They both singled out the boy for special praise, and Simeon declared that Jesus was the Messiah. This incident is used by Luke to prove that Jesus would initiate a new era and new teaching. The fact that Simeon could die in peace after he saw Jesus was also a symbol of the passing away of the old Jewish covenant with God and the beginning of something new with Christ.

Tradition says that this is the spot where Jesus was born. Today this is inside the Church of the Nativity in Bethlehem.

The prayer of praise which Simeon makes in verses 29-32 is called the **Nunc Dimittis**. It contains three main points:

1 Simeon could die in peace as Jesus, the Messiah, had arrived.
2 Jesus would bring salvation.
3 Jesus' message would be for both Jews and Gentiles. (This is known as **universalism.**)

The boy Jesus in the Temple

Luke 2:39-52

The Temple was the centre of celebrations at festival times during the Jewish year. On this occasion of **Passover**, the most important of the Jewish festivals, thousands of people would have been gathered in Jerusalem and it would not have been difficult for a child to get lost. It is probable that Luke singles out this event in Jesus' boyhood, when he was twelve, as it was the age of **Bar Mitzvah** – the ceremony at which a Jewish boy becomes an adult. As we can see from the account, Luke also suggests that at this time Jesus was becoming more aware of his own identity and special relationship to God.

Throughout the whole of chapters 1 and 2, Luke emphasises again and again that Mary and Joseph are doing everything that "was required by the law of the Lord"; in other words they carried out all the Jewish customs and traditions associated with bringing up a child.

***Bar Mitzvah** means 'son of the Law'. A boy must prepare himself for his Bar Mitzvah by attending special classes given by a rabbi who teaches him how to read or recite passages from the Law. On the day of his Bar Mitzvah the boy takes his place with the men of the synagogue. During the service he is called to the front to read parts of the Law aloud. Once this is over the boy becomes a full member of the Jewish community. In modern Jewish synagogues there is also a ceremony for girls. This is called a **Bat Mitzvah**.*

This Jewish boy lives in Jerusalem and his Bar Mitzvah is taking place out of doors at the Wailing Wall which is a place of great significance for the Jewish people. Do you remember what the Wailing Wall is? Find out why it is called this.

Questions

1 What are the 'birth narratives'?
2 a) Joseph intended to divorce Mary. What made him change his mind?
b) What kind of a person must Joseph have been?
3 What do the following names mean:
a) Jesus b) Immanuel?
4 Why does Matthew refer to many Old Testament prophecies when telling the birth story?
5 Why was it significant that Jesus was born in Bethlehem?
6 In the Magnificat, what was Mary's attitude to
a) herself?
b) God?
7 What part do ordinary and underprivileged people play in the birth narratives?
8 Select two of the gifts which the visitors from the East gave to Jesus and explain how they would relate to future events in his life.
9 What symbolic significance do Simeon and Anna have in Luke's birth narrative?
10 What three important Jewish traditions did Jesus and his parents participate in during his childhood?
11 What is a Bar Mitzvah?

Activity

1 Angels, dreams and visions play a very important rôle in the birth narratives. In pairs, look over the texts in this chapter and list all the times they occur, and their significance. The grid below is an example of how you could set out your work:

REFERENCE	*DREAM/ VISION/ANGEL*	*PURPOSE*
Mt 1:20	*Angel appears to Joseph*	*Tells him to marry Mary and call baby 'Jesus'*
Lk 1:28	*Angel appears to Mary*	*Tells her she will have a virgin birth*

2 Look at the references to Jesus' birth in Matthew's gospel. Make a list of the prophesies from the Old Testament which he believes were fulfilled.

Baptism & Temptation

The baptism of Jesus

Matthew 3:1-17

In this passage John the Baptist is described like an Old Testament **prophet**. The popular image of a prophet is of someone who simply made predictions about the future. In fact, a prophet was a person who explained God's word for the present and how to act it out.

Occasionally they suggested what the consequences of not following their advice would be, but it was not a type of fortune telling.

Often, prophets were outspoken and offended people; John did this too. He called the religious leaders 'snakes' and said they were like trees which would be cut down and thrown into a fire.

Matthew believed that John the Baptist was just like the prophet Elijah – a second Elijah. The evidence for this is in Matthew 17:12-13. Jesus said:

"Elijah has already come, and they did not recognise him."

The disciples understood that he was talking about John the Baptist.

Another clue that John was a second Elijah was his dress, which was almost identical to Elijah's. (Compare 2 Kings 1:8 with Matthew 3:4.)

John's role in this event was to baptise Jesus. Baptism was not a new idea; there is evidence that the Essenes used baptism at their Qumran community as a type of ritual cleansing.

In John's case the purpose of baptism was to show an outward sign of repentance, a way of saying sorry to God and making a fresh start. But he made it clear that this was an inferior baptism compared to one to come – baptism with the Holy Spirit and fire.

Baptism literally means 'to dip', but there is an ongoing debate as to whether baptism involves the whole body being immersed in water or a sprinkling of water over the head.

It seems that John was reluctant to baptise Jesus because he thought he was not worthy to do the job, and because he didn't think that Jesus needed to repent from his sins as he was perfect.

Eventually he agreed and the baptism took place. It was accompanied by three significant events:

- The Heavens opened.
- The Spirit of God appeared.
- A voice from heaven spoke.

Notice that the dove in verse 16 was a symbol of the Holy Spirit and with that power Jesus was equipped to carry out his ministry. Also, the voice from heaven affirmed Jesus' identity in similar words to those used by Jesus himself when he had visited the Temple as a child. This was another occasion when Jesus' divine identity was glimpsed.

Some Christians believe that on each of these important occasions Jesus was gradually becoming more aware of his own identity and purpose in life. However, other Christians disagree and say that Jesus was always fully aware of his divine nature, and it was other people who understood it gradually.

The temptation of Jesus

Matthew 4:1-11

After his baptism Jesus took time to think about what had happened and what lay ahead. He spent forty days in the desert during which he was tempted. Matthew says that 'The devil came to him.'

Christians don't generally imagine that a physical devil was present, certainly not one that was all red with horns and a tail! Also, it is thought that Jesus faced more than just three temptations. The gospel account is therefore a picture or image of a mental struggle during which Jesus had to resolve to take the difficult path, turning his back on the easy options which would have led him into evil.

The three temptations which Matthew tells us about give us an insight into issues which Jesus was wrestling with during his forty days.

1 **'Order these stones to turn into bread'**
The first dilemma which Jesus faced was how to use his miraculous power – should he use it for selfish reasons or in order to help others? Jesus denied himself that opportunity to satisfy his hunger, even though he had been fasting for forty days. This shows that he is not concerned with material things but with spiritual food given by God.

2 **'Throw yourself down'**
Jesus was told to throw himself from the Temple, and on this one occasion the Devil himself quoted scripture. Again, the challenge to Jesus was to misuse his power, but it also asked Jesus to prove that he was the Messiah and that God really cared for him. This question was an important one for Jesus to deal with because he would be faced with it again and again as people questioned his authority and identity.

3 **'Kneel down and worship me'**
This temptation tested Jesus' devotion to God and also his desire for political power. Would he be able to refuse control over the whole earth? But Jesus showed that his vision of a Messiah was not one who had political power, but one who put God's kingdom first.

The response

Jesus' responses to these temptations all came in the form of quotations from the Old Testament book Deuteronomy. Look them up for yourself:

- Deuteronomy 8:3
- Deuteronomy 6:16
- Deuteronomy 6:13

They are commands given to the nation of Israel by God after their escape from Egypt. However, the Israelites went on to break the commandments by:

- grumbling to God about not having enough food;
- testing God and doubting his ability to support them;
- worshipping other gods.

So, in this account Matthew is not just explaining how Jesus strengthened himself against temptations, but also how he succeeded at every point in which the Israelites failed.

As a result of the temptations Jesus was stronger and more prepared for beginning his ministry because he had rejected three false ways of doing his task:

a) providing only for the material needs of men and women;
b) using his power to do miraculous tricks and win popularity;
c) giving in to evil in order to gain political power.

Questions

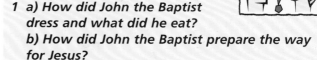

***1** a) How did John the Baptist dress and what did he eat?*
b) How did John the Baptist prepare the way for Jesus?
***2** a) Why was John reluctant to baptise Jesus?*
b) Why do you think Jesus wanted to be baptised?
***3** a) In which river was Jesus baptised?*
b) Describe what happened when Jesus was baptised.
***4** a) Where did the Temptations take place?*
b) For how long was Jesus tempted?
***5** In which temptation did Satan quote scripture?*
***6** Explain how the temptations represent three ways in which Jesus could have chosen to do his work as the Messiah wrongly.*
***7** In what ways are we tempted today to be dependent on material things?*

Activity

***a** In groups, use the following headings to make a list of ways in which young people today are tempted to be:*

GREEDY	*ENVIOUS*
SEXUALLY PERMISSIVE	*LAZY*
DISOBEDIENT TO PARENTS	*DISHONEST*

***b** Discuss what Christians might learn from the example of Jesus about how to deal with these temptations.*

LENT IS WHAT YOU DO

TRÓCAIRE

Catholic and Anglican Christians remember Jesus' temptations in the wilderness during the season of Lent. It is a time of reflection and they are encouraged to give up something they like to remind them of Jesus' fasting and suffering. Do you think the Trocaire slogan is effective? Explain why.

Jesus' Identity is Questioned

In this section we will look at several texts in which people showed their amazement at who Jesus was and what he did. The Jews had formed various ideas about what the Messiah would be like. They thought he would have some or all of the qualities of:

- a priest
- a king
- a military leader.

But Jesus did not fit into any of these moulds and people found it difficult to know what to expect of him. Religious leaders were shocked and surprised at his words and actions. So were his disciples and even friends and neighbours who had grown up with him in Nazareth.

Jesus calms a storm

Matthew 8:23-27

During a storm on the Sea of Galilee, Jesus' disciples thought they were about to die, but Jesus showed his authority and ordered the storm to stop. They were amazed at his power over nature, something which his disciples would have associated only with prophets like Moses, who with God's power had control over the Red Sea. They wondered, therefore, what Jesus' true identity was – a prophet, the Messiah or God himself? This incident also demonstrated the importance of faith to the disciples.

Jesus calls Matthew

Matthew 9:9-13

In this episode Jesus' identity as a religious teacher was brought into question. According to Jewish law a Jew could not associate with outcasts as they were considered 'unclean'. This was not a physical dirtiness but meant someone who was religiously impure. People who were considered outcasts included those with skin diseases (lepers), prostitutes, criminals and tax collectors.

Looking across the Sea of Galilee towards the town of Tiberius.

With the question 'Why do you eat with tax collectors and other outcasts?' Jesus' identity was again brought under the spotlight. His reply demonstrated that he was unlike any other religious teacher as they were concerned with animal sacrifices and other religious duties but he was concerned with the poor and marginalised people of society. To help everyone to understand this, Jesus used an everyday example – doctors are not needed for those who are in good health, but for the sick.

Jesus is rejected at Nazareth

Matthew 13:53-58

The people of Jesus' home town were not at all impressed by Jesus' teaching, parables and miracles. As far as they were concerned Jesus was only 'the carpenter's son', and any other image he had of himself was nonsense. Christians today believe that Jesus was both human and divine, but his friends and neighbours from Nazareth could only see the human side. Jesus quoted what might have been a proverb: 'A prophet is respected everywhere except in his home town and by his own family' (v57).

This passage also gives us some extra information about Jesus' family. The Good News Bible says he had three brothers: Joseph, Simon and Judas and several sisters, whose names we are not told. The Catholic Church believes that this translation is inaccurate, however, because Mary was a 'perpetual virgin', which means she did not have any children before or after Jesus. They believe that the brothers and sisters of Jesus mentioned here were in fact close relations of Jesus – perhaps cousins – and that their mother was another Mary, mentioned again by Matthew in chapter 27:56.

Questions

1 ***What everyday example did Jesus use to explain 'I have not come to call the righteous, but sinners'?***
2 ***Explain in your own words how Jesus' identity was questioned by:***
a) Disciples b) Religious Leaders c) Friends and neighbours.

Activity

Draw a spider diagram, like the one below, and in groups try to jot down all the questions you or other people today might have about Jesus' identity.

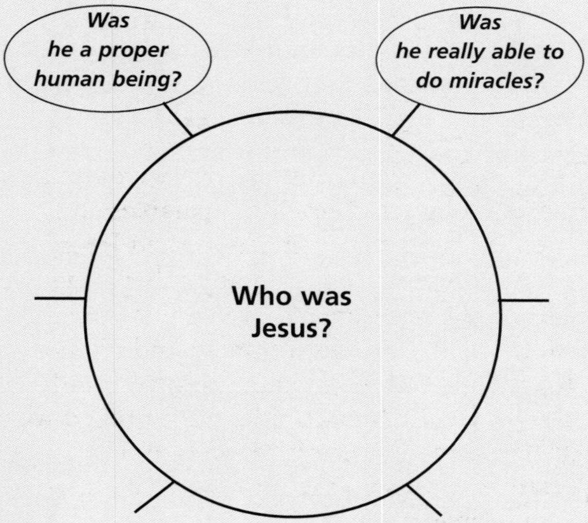
Was he a proper human being?
Was he really able to do miracles?
Who was Jesus?

Titles of Jesus

Activity

Before you begin reading this chapter, try to make a list of different titles that people have. You might think about titles used by professional people, politicians or royalty. In each case the titles you have listed should tell you something about what the person does or who they are.

In the New Testament there are several titles associated with Jesus which help us when trying to come to an understanding of his identity.

1 *Son of Man*

Matthew 9:1-8
Jesus heals a paralysed man

The significance of this incident lies in two main phrases used by Jesus:

"Courage, my son! Your sins are forgiven."

and

"I will prove to you, then, that the Son of Man has authority on earth to forgive sins."

By healing this paralysed man and by forgiving his sins Jesus proved that he had the power to heal both physically and spiritually. The Pharisees considered his words **blasphemy** (speaking against God) because in their eyes, only God could forgive sins, so Jesus was claiming equality with God. Jesus, however, did not call himself God but Son of Man. This title has more than one meaning:

a) simply *a man.*

b) a *suffering servant.* In other gospels Jesus used this phrase when he was referring to the suffering that he would experience. Some New Testament scholars have linked this with the Old Testament idea of the Suffering Servant:

"He endured the suffering that should have been ours, the pain that we should have borne."
(Isaiah 53:4)

c) *one who has authority.*

The title Son of Man is also used in the Old Testament book of Daniel where he is described as a person who will have 'authority, honour and royal power' and a kingdom which would never end (Daniel 7:14). This image is also referred to in Matthew 16:27.

So this title sums up the dual identity of Jesus: he was both a man who experienced suffering, and a divine king who is eternal and who has authority and power.

2 *Son of David*

The title Son of David was a double compliment as:

a) it described Jesus in royal terms because it linked him with the greatest and most successful king the Jewish people ever had.
b) it was believed that the Messiah would be a descendant of David's family.

So the title was saying that Jesus would be as great a leader as David and was the Messiah.

Matthew 9:27-34
Jesus heals two blind men

On this occasion Jesus healed two blind men, but he did not want them to tell anyone about what he had done. This was typical of Jesus' attitude to those whom he healed or to those who said that he was the Messiah. This secrecy about his identity may have been for two reasons:

- He did not want to be known simply as a miracle worker.
- He did not want to be known as the Son of David or Messiah as he was not the type of Messiah people expected and it would have confused them.

Immediately after Jesus healed the blind men he was confronted by a demon-possessed man who could not speak, and he healed him as well. The Pharisees were angry at everything he had done and hurled insults at him. Their opinion was that Jesus was not the Son of David but the prince of demons.

Matthew 15:21-28
A woman's faith

In this second example where Matthew uses the title Son of David, a woman asked for her daughter to be healed of an evil spirit. The response which Jesus made to the woman is rather perplexing as Jesus seemed to suggest that he would not heal her because she was a Gentile. He even went so far as to compare her to a dog who did not deserve to be given something which was not hers. It could easily be concluded that this is an example of prejudice! However, there are two possible explanations why Jesus said these words:

a) It is possible that Jesus was speaking with irony, mocking the views of the religious leaders who would have believed that he should not help this woman because they regarded the Gentiles as being 'unclean'.
b) Jesus was testing the woman's faith to see if she truly believed that *all* people were welcome in the Kingdom of God.

Whatever we make of his words, Jesus believed the woman had faith and healed her daughter. By doing this he also demonstrated that all people have a place in God's Kingdom.

3 *Son of God*

Matthew 14:22-23
Jesus walks on the water

Again the disciples found themselves on a boat in a storm, but this time Jesus was not with them; he had decided to stay on the shore. According to Matthew, in the early hours of the morning Jesus showed his power over nature by walking on water. Peter asked Jesus if he too could walk on the water but because he felt afraid and lacked faith he was not able to go more than a couple of steps.

This is one of several occasions when Peter is singled out from the other disciples. This highlights his importance in the early church at the time when Matthew was writing his gospel. At the end of the experience the disciples concluded: "Truly you are the Son of God".

This title, Son of God, would not have been unfamiliar to people of that time. Many of the Greek gods had this title and kings or emperors sometimes called themselves Sons of God. So Matthew's task was to explain to his readers through Jesus' actions and words what the title Son of God really meant. On this occasion he shows that Jesus, the Son of God, is able to save and able to do miracles.

4 *Christ/Messiah*

Matthew 16:13-20
Peter's declaration about Christ

Eventually, Jesus brought the subject of his identity into the open by asking directly: "Who do you think the Son of Man is?" The disciples reported that people said he was John the Baptist, Elijah, Jeremiah or another prophet, but Peter was quite clear about his opinion:
"You are the Messiah, the Son of the living God".

The title **Messiah** is the Hebrew version of the Greek word **Christ**. They both mean 'anointed one', or 'one chosen by God'. When someone was made a king or priest they were anointed with a small amount of oil. The Jews anticipated that a Messiah would be sent by God in the future to make them a great nation once again. They thought he would have the qualities of a prophet, a priest and a king.

In reply to Peter's declaration, Jesus praised him and stated that he was the rock on which Christ's church would be built. These words of Jesus have caused division among Christians right up to the present day. Jesus seemed to state that Peter was the foundation of his church, he had been given the keys of the Kingdom of Heaven and what he permitted or prohibited on earth would be permitted or prohibited in heaven.

The Roman Catholic Church teaches that at Caesarea Philippi, Peter was made the first Pope or leader of the Church and the keys are a symbol of the authority which Peter was given. This authority, Catholics believe, has been passed down through generation after generation of Popes, right down to the present day. The right to permit or prohibit things on heaven or earth, they believe, refers to the Pope's power to forgive sin, make statements about Church doctrine and reach decisions about Church discipline.

Protestant Christians disagree with this interpretation and suggest that when Jesus said 'this rock' he was not in fact speaking about Peter but about his statement "You are the Messiah, the Son of the living God". They also point to the Gospel of John where Jesus gave the authority to forgive sins to all the apostles, not just to Peter (John 20:22-23).

Questions

1 *Why were the religious leaders offended by Jesus healing the paralysed man?*
2 *Jesus was referred to as the 'Son of Man'. Why was this a good title?*
3 *a) Outline one occasion when Jesus was called the 'Son of David'.*
b) What special significance did this title have?
4 *a) Why could Jesus' response to the Canaanite woman be regarded as offensive?*
b) In your opinion, why did Jesus act in this way?
5 *a) Who tried to walk on water to reach Jesus, and why was he not able to go more than a couple of steps?*
b) What did the disciples call Jesus on this occasion?
6 *a) What two questions did Jesus ask his disciples at Caesarea Philippi?*
b) What did Simon Peter say in answer to the second question?
7 *What does the Roman Catholic Church understand about Jesus' teaching in Matthew 16:17-19?*

The Transfiguration

Matthew 17:1-9 ✓

The word **transfiguration** means a change in the aspect of something or someone, making it more spiritual or important. At the Transfiguration, Jesus experienced a change in appearance by becoming 'like the sun' and he was elevated to a position of importance equal to the two Old Testament figures, Moses and Elijah. Moses represented the Law and Elijah the Prophets. This suggests that Jesus was their successor and fulfilled their prophecies.

A shining cloud also descended, and a voice was heard saying 'This is my Son with whom I am pleased.' This is similar to the voice at Jesus' baptism (see p 21). In the Old Testament a cloud was a symbol of God's presence. For example in Exodus 24:15-18; 40:34, the dazzling light of God's presence appeared to Moses in a cloud.

The reaction of the disciples was one of fear, and Peter seemed to be so shocked that he didn't know what to say. He suggested marking the spot where Jesus spoke with Moses and Elijah by building three tents for them to stay in. This may have been a reference to the feast of the tabernacles during which Jews put up tents.

Jesus in Jerusalem

The triumphant entry

Matthew 21:1-11

By this stage Jesus was no longer concerned about keeping his identity a secret. As we can see from Matthew's description of this occasion, Jesus organised the public procession himself (v2-4). So Jesus was confirming his true identity, that he was:

- the Messiah predicted in the Old Testament scriptures;
- the Son of David;
- a humble servant (he rode a colt, not a horse as a king would have done);
- a man popular with the ordinary people, not regarded as a hypocrite like other religious leaders.

Christians today remember Jesus' entry to Jerusalem on **Palm Sunday**. In the Anglican and Catholic Church it is usual to receive a palm cross.

Jesus goes to the Temple

Matthew 21:12-17

If you look back to page 11 you will be able to see what the Temple in Jerusalem might have been like during the time of Jesus. The area Jesus would have entered on this occasion was the Court of the Gentiles, because this is where it was usual to buy and sell animal sacrifices and change money. Worshippers could only sacrifice animals which had been inspected by the Temple officials, so they bought them in the Temple courts, but the traders there charged ten or fifteen times more for their inspected animals than an animal from a normal market.

Everyone also had to pay a Temple tax, but it had to be paid in Galilean shekels as other coins which bore the portrait of a leader were unacceptable because they broke the second commandment:

"Do not make for yourselves images of anything in heaven, or on earth."

So money had to be changed and money changers charged a large fee for doing so. Jesus was outraged that people were being exploited, particularly in a place that should have been for prayer.

On page 50 you can see a film maker's idea of what happened. Of course, by turning over their tables Jesus infuriated the traders and the religious leaders, but their anger became even worse when he healed people and the people called him the Son of David. Jesus accepted this title, which was blasphemy to the Pharisees, as it made Jesus out to be the Messiah.

Discussion

1. ***Do you think that church buildings should be used for activities other than worship?***
2. ***Are there some activities which you would consider to be inappropriate in a church building?***

Questions

1. ***Name the disciples who were with Jesus at the Transfiguration.***
2. ***Name ONE change which took place in Jesus' appearance at the Transfiguration.***
3. ***Why did Elijah and Moses appear with Jesus?***
4. ***a) What did the voice from the cloud say at the Transfiguration?***
   b) After what other event in the life of Jesus were similar words spoken about him?
5. ***What did Peter want to do to mark the occasion?***
6. ***What New Testament character was Jesus referring to when he spoke about Elijah?***
7. ***a) How did Jesus enter Jerusalem in Matthew 21?***
   b) In what ways did Jesus' entry into Jerusalem represent a) his humility, and b) his importance?
8. ***a) What did Jesus say to the traders in the Temple?***
   b) Explain how the traders in the Temple were exploiting the worshippers.

King of Kings, MGM, 1961

The Teachings of Jesus

Jesus was a **rabbi**, a teacher, who like the prophets before him tried to communicate God's message to the world. Jesus' teaching was practical and challenging; he used simple stories with familiar activities, characters and locations which his listeners warmed to. He was also direct and serious in the points he was trying to get across. In this unit we will examine Jesus' teaching on discipleship, prayer, forgiveness, wealth and poverty, humility and ambition, and life after death.

Parables

Much of the teaching Jesus gave was through parables. A parable could be described as a simple story which illustrates a spiritual truth about the Kingdom of God. The benefits of using parables as a teaching method were:

1. Parables were a common method of teaching at the time of Jesus. The people would have felt comfortable listening to them because they were familiar.
2. Parables were simple stories. They were easy to remember and would have been appreciated by a wide audience.
3. Parables challenged the people to work out the meaning for themselves. Those who took the time to do this were the ones for whom the parables were told.
4. Parables showed people that Jesus understood and appreciated their lives. Jesus could relate to his listeners.
5. Parables were interesting and caught the audience's attention.

Discipleship

All rabbis had **disciples** who learned from their teaching and tried to follow in their footsteps. In the examples we will be studying it is clear that Jesus' disciples had a lot to learn and at times they had great difficulty in understanding what they were being taught. Christians today also see themselves as disciples of Jesus and try to live as closely as possible to his teaching.

Salt and light

Matthew 5:13-16

Jesus taught that his followers should be like salt. Salt both preserves and flavours food and only a small amount has a large effect. However, salt that has lost its saltiness or flavour is useless. In the same way Jesus meant that Christians who have lost their commitment to God are also useless. They will have no effect on the world around them.

Jesus expanded this idea by saying that Christians should be like light. Because the world is in darkness, their faith must shine out so that others will be interested in Christianity. Their faith could shine in two ways: by what they say and by what they do. Jesus meant that if his followers did not set a good example then they would be as ineffective as a light that is hidden under a bowl.

Christians today can show their faith by acting in a Christ-like way or by taking a moral stand on many different issues, for example: unfairness, poverty, or when life is threatened. A practical faith is called for if Christians are to shine like lights.

The cost of being a Disciple

Luke 14:25-33

Jesus demanded total commitment from his disciples. He clearly stated that God should be first in their lives, above everything else. Therefore, Jesus explained, a person should not become a disciple until they weighed up all the costs. This may even have meant being prepared to face death for the sake of the gospel: "Whoever does not carry his own cross and come after me cannot be my disciple." (v27)

Jesus told two parables to illustrate the importance of preparing carefully before taking a major decision:

1) Before building a tower it is necessary to work out if you can afford it, otherwise you may be laughed at for not being able to finish the job.
2) Similarly, a king going to war with another king will, first of all, work out if he is strong enough for battle. If not, he will make peace with his enemy.

Jesus concluded his teaching by saying that those people who became disciples but who weren't able to cope with the demands of discipleship were as worthless as salt that was no longer salty and had to be thrown away.

Christians today believe that if they allow their faith to fade they too will be like a ruined builder, a conquered king or spoiled salt.

Activity

Try to think of someone who has shown a Christian example to others. They might be a famous person (in the past or present) or someone in your community. There are some suggestions below of places you might find information. Find out as much as you can about the person and then explain to the rest of your class how the person has been "salt" and "light" to the world around them.

Resources

- ***Read examples of modern disciples from the "Faith In Action" series published by RMEP, for example:***
  'In the Streets of Calcutta' (Mother Teresa)
  'Free at Last' (Martin Luther King)
  'Helen' (Helen Keller)
  'No Compromise' Dietrich Bonhoeffer
- ***Look up resources on the internet eg:***
  www.tisv.be/mt/indmt.htm
  www.cyberword.com/bonhoef/
  www.wagingpeace.org
  www.seattletimes.com/mlk/index.html
  www.at.nobel.se/laureates/peace-1984-1-bio.html

An example of an unstable foundation! Mussenden Temple, near Downhill in Co Londonderry is now so near the edge of a crumbling cliff that the National Trust has had to reinforce the cliff face to stop the Temple falling into the sea.

The two housebuilders

Matthew 7:24-29

The weather and house-building are the two everyday topics which Jesus used in this parable. Palestine had many areas of desert and the need for a good foundation when building a house was essential if it was to stand up to the heavy seasonal rains.

Jesus explained that anyone who hears his words and acts on them was like a wise man who built his house on rock; that is, nothing would destroy his faith. However, if he heard Jesus' words and did not act on them he was like a foolish man who built his house on sand – his faith would be washed away.

The rain in this parable is a symbol of things which threaten a Christian's faith, for example, persecution, loss of health or the death of a close friend or relative. Jesus explained that it was the person who maintained obedience to his teaching in the face of hardship who would have a foundation of faith which can overcome testing.

The crowd were amazed at Jesus teaching because he wasn't like the teachers of the law; instead he spoke with authority.

The parable of the sower

Matthew 13:1-23

This parable is about the Kingdom of God. This is a central theme in all the gospels. Matthew called it 'The Kingdom of Heaven' – probably because he was a Jew and wanted to avoid using God's name out of respect for the third commandment. However, they both refer to the same thing.

When we think of the word 'kingdom' we usually assume it is referring to a place, but Jesus' understanding of the Kingdom of God was that it was a people – those who put God's rule first in their lives.

When Jesus began his work in Galilee (Matthew 4:12-17) he preached:
"Turn away from your sins because the Kingdom of God is near."

In effect he was proclaiming that God's rule had come.

Matthew chapter 13 outlines seven parables of the Kingdom. Here we are going to look at one of them in detail: the parable of the sower. This is one of the most famous parables told by Jesus. Matthew writes about this parable in **3 parts:**

1 Chapter 13:1-9 The parable of the sower; told to a large crowd.

"Once there was a man who went out to sow corn"

Jesus said that preaching the good news about God is like sowing seed. Sometimes it takes root and sometimes it doesn't.

Here is Rev Donald Soper, later Lord Soper, a famous Methodist preacher pictured at Speaker's Corner, Hyde Park in London where he went every Sunday afternoon for many years. He died in 1998 at the age of 95.

He attracted hecklers and loved to debate with those who stood around to listen. He called this 'the fellowship of controversy'. Once, a man called out that Christianity had been around for two thousand years and the state of the world was no better. Donald Soper replied: "Soap has been around for a long time and look at the state of your neck!"

2 Chapter 13:10-17 The purpose of parables; told privately to the disciples.

3 Chapter 13:18-24 An explanation of the parable of the sower given by Jesus privately to the disciples.

The parable of the sower is a special type of parable which is called an **allegory**.

What is an allegory?

An allegory is a type of parable where the characters and events all represent real people and events. Every detail in an allegory has a meaning. This is where an allegory is different from other parables. A simple parable makes one point and the listeners work out the meaning for themselves.

In order to understand the full meaning of the parable, the chart on the next page shows parts one and three alongside each other as well as a column suggesting how Christians today might apply the lessons of the parable in their own lives.

The purpose of parables

Matthew 13:10-17

After hearing the parable of the sower (v1-9), the disciples asked Jesus "Why do you use parables when you talk to the people?"

Jesus replied that, because his disciples had faith, then the meaning behind his parables came easily to them but the majority of Jesus' listeners refused his message so the parables remained confusing to them.

Verse twelve highlights the fact that those who easily understood the truths about God's kingdom, and sought to know more, would progress to understand more. But those with hard, proud, unbelieving hearts, those who did not seek God, would never understand even a little. Christians today agree that those who continually reject God's word will never understand it.

Jesus' statement in verse thirteen seems to suggest that he taught in parables to confuse

[go to page 35

The Parable	Meaning	Implications for today
v3 "Once there was a man who went out to sow corn."	**Man** = God **Corn seed** = The Word of God	The Word of God is like seed because when planted in people's hearts new spiritual life grows. The parable teaches what will happen to the Word of God when it is proclaimed.
v4 "As he scattered the seed in the field, some of it fell along the path and the birds ate it up."	**Path** = "Those who hear the message about the Kingdom but do not understand it." (v19). **Birds** = "The Evil One comes along and snatches away what was sown in them." (v19)	Some people are distracted from taking Christianity seriously.
v5-6 "Some of it fell on rocky ground, where there was little soil. The seeds soon sprouted, because the soil wasn't deep. But when the sun came up, it burnt the young plants; and because the roots had not grown deep enough, the plants soon dried up."	**Rocky ground** = "Those who receive the message gladly as soon as they hear it. But it does not sink deep into them, and they don't last long." (v20-21) **Sun** = "So when trouble or persecution comes along because of the message, they give up at once." (v22)	Some people are attracted by Christianity until they realise that it requires a deep commitment. Friends may laugh at them or cut them off so they give up.
v7 "Some of the seed fell among thorn bushes, which grew up and choked the plants."	**Thorn bushes** ="Those who hear the message; but the worries about this life and the love for riches choke the message and they don't bear fruit." (v22)	Some people may allow worries about work, family or money to destroy God's influence in their lives. 'Thorns' could also be compared to greed, anger or jealousy, all of which choke spiritual growth.
v8 "But some seed fell in good soil, and the plants produced corn, some produced a hundred grains, others sixty, and others thirty"	**Good soil** = "Those who hear the message and understand it: they bear fruit, some as much as a hundred, others sixty, others thirty." (v23)	A minority will accept the message and remain firm in their faith in spite of difficulties which they may face. They will go on to grow as Christians, fulfilling God's purpose in their lives.

people deliberately and prevent them from understanding his true message, but some scholars think it may be Matthew's way of explaining why those to whom Jesus preached did not all respond.

The quotation from Isaiah's prophecy (see Isaiah 6:9-10) backs up Jesus' statement. In the Old Testament Isaiah received his commission to be a prophet to the people of Israel but he was warned that they would not pay attention to him. If anything, the more he spoke to them, the more they would ignore him and turn away from his message. Jesus was facing the same situation. Unless people had repentant hearts and were sincere in listening to him, they would never understand the parables. By teaching in parables, Jesus could work out who was willing to hear the gospel and who was hard and proud to his teaching.

The purpose which Jesus had in telling the parable of the sower was to show that God's word would be accepted by different people in different ways. It also illustrates that those who follow Christ will experience hardships and difficulties but, despite these, the Kingdom of God will succeed.

A brother or sister who sins

Matthew 18:15-20

This passage is the only place where the Gospels speak of the 'Church'. As far as we know, Jesus never established any churches so here Matthew must be applying Jesus' teaching on discipline to the Church of his own time. Clear guidelines on how to deal with those who sinned were essential to the smooth running of the early Christian communities. Matthew outlines four steps to be taken.

1 If someone sees a fellow Christian sin then it is their duty to try to put the matter right in private.

2 If this does not work, then a few witnesses should be taken along. This was in keeping with the Old Testament law:

"One man is not enough to convict a man of a crime: at least two witnesses are necessary to prove that a man is guilty."

Deuteronomy 19:15

The purpose of this is to bring about a reconciliation.

3 Failing that, the whole thing should be told to the local church, but publicity should be avoided if possible.

4 If the offender refuses to accept the Church's verdict then he should be treated as though he were a tax collector or pagan, ie, excluded from the life of the church. The purpose is not to destroy the offender's faith but to bring him to repentance.

Questions

1 *a) Explain what Jesus meant when he said that his disciples should be like 'salt' and 'light'.*
b) Give your opinion on how Christians might set a good example:
at home
at school
in the wider community.

2 *a) In what way can a person's faith be challenged today?*
b) How might Jesus' teaching in the parable of the house-builders help such a person?

3 *a) Give an account of the parable of the sower (Matthew13:1-9).*
b) In your opinion, is this parable still relevant today? Give reasons for your answer.

4 *Do you think it is difficult for people to accept God's word today? You might use some of the following in your answer:*
– the power of the media
– busy work schedules
– importance of the church
– youth organisations
– drugs and dance culture

5 *"Parables were a successful teaching method at the time of Jesus but have lost their impact in the modern world." Do you agree or disagree with this statement? Give reasons for your answer.*

6 *Do you think Jesus' teaching on "a brother or sister who sins" has any relevance for the church today?*

7 *Using evidence from the Bible, explain what you consider to be the qualities of a true disciple of Christ.*

8 *How do you think Christians carry their own cross today?*

Prayer

Activity

Carry out a quick survey of opinions in your class on prayer:

a) How many people pray?

b) How many pray more than once a week?

c) How many pray only in a time of crisis?

d) How many people think that prayer is important?

Teaching about prayer

Matthew 6:5-15

Jesus began his teaching on prayer here by saying how not to pray:

1 **Don't show-off**. Synagogues were places of worship where many people gathered to pray. Jesus spoke against those who prayed loudly just so they could be seen and praised by others. He called such people **hypocrites**, that is, people whose actions and words contradict each other – people who do not practise what they preach. True Christians are those who pray when no-one else is around. Again, God will reward them appropriately.

2 **Don't use a lot of meaningless words**. The Gentiles' prayers were long because they thought that this practice would impress their many gods. Jesus taught that his followers did not need to be like that because God knows what they need before they ask.

The Lord's Prayer

Matthew 6:9-13

Jesus gave his followers a model for all prayer. Throughout history Christians have repeated this prayer and today it is still recited in churches, schools, and at Christian gatherings throughout the world. It unites people in their faith and gives them something common to focus on when so much attempts to drive them apart. It is commonly known as 'The Lord's Prayer' or the 'Our Father' and it sums up Jesus' teaching about the Kingdom of God:

v9 "Our Father in Heaven"

When Jesus prayed to God, he used the word 'Abba' which means 'daddy'. He wanted to show that God is as approachable as a loving father who wants the best for his children. At the same time, God is in heaven so he must be approached with an appropriate measure of reverence and awe.

v9 "May your holy name be honoured."

Jesus' words showed that it is important to put God's glory first before his followers come to their own personal needs.

**v10 "May your kingdom come.
May your will be done on earth as it is in heaven."**

Christians believe when Jesus came as a man, God's kingdom came to the world. Wherever the Kingdom of God is, God's will is being fulfilled. In this prayer Jesus urged his followers to pray that God's kingdom would reach its potential on earth.

v11 "Give us today the food we need."

As well as physical food and good health, Jesus taught that people need to satisfy their emotional and spiritual needs. The prayer suggests that God will supply this help each day as it is needed.

v12 "Forgive us the wrongs we have done, as we forgive the wrongs that others have done to us."

Jesus reminded his followers that only those who were prepared to forgive could ask for forgiveness. This is part and parcel of being a Christian.

v13 "Do not bring us to hard testing, but deliver us from the evil one."

This can perhaps better be translated "Lead us not into temptation." It is a plea that Jesus' followers will not give in to the temptations they face. 'The evil one' refers to Satan who seeks to destroy a Christian's faith.

Note: Many Greeks manuscripts add the words:
"For yours is the kingdom, the power and the glory, forever and ever. Amen."

v14-15 Comment on Forgiveness

At the end of the prayer Jesus reinforced the idea that God's forgiveness is dependent upon his followers forgiveness of each other.

Types of prayer

In the Lord's Prayer we can identify different types of prayer:

1 Praise – a prayer in which Christians express adoration to God.

2 Confession – a prayer in which Christians admit they have sinned and ask for forgiveness.

3 Thanksgiving – a prayer in which Christians thank God for what he has done in their lives.

4 Petition – a prayer in which Christians ask God for what they need in their lives.

5 Intercession – a prayer in which Christians ask God for what other people need in their lives.

Discussion

In groups discuss whether you think it is a good idea to say the Lord's Prayer in a school assembly or classroom.
After you have discussed you opinions, organise a class debate on the statement: "The daily repetition of prayers makes them meaningless and insignificant".

Forgiveness

As well as teaching about forgiveness through the Lord's Prayer, Jesus gave practical guidelines and clear examples of how he expected his followers to act in a forgiving way.

The parable of the unforgiving servant

Matthew 18:21-35

Peter asked Jesus about forgiveness:

"Lord, if my brother keeps on sinning against me, how many times do I have to forgive him? Seven times?"

(v21)

In Bible times the number seven meant completeness or perfection. So to forgive seven times would be very commendable indeed. Jesus' reply enforced the Christian duty of unlimited forgiveness:

"No, not seven times but seventy times seven."

Jesus then went on to illustrate his answer by a parable which revealed more truths about the Kingdom of Heaven.

A servant owed a king 'millions of pounds' which he could never repay even if he was sold as a slave, along with his wife and family. He would never pay off such a colossal debt. The servant went to the king and promised an impossible task: to repay the king everything. The king, knowing this was impossible, felt sorry for him and cancelled the debt. The size of the debt showed the extent of the forgiveness.

However, the forgiven servant quickly forgot what the king had done for him and failed to learn from the king's example. After leaving the palace, the servant met a fellow servant who owed him only a few pounds. The first servant refused to be patient with him and threw him into jail. On hearing this, the king immediately withdrew his forgiveness from the unmerciful servant. He reinstated the debt and put him into jail until he paid it back. This was impossible for the first servant to do.

Jesus stressed that this is exactly what God will do to those who will not forgive from the heart. In other words, if Christians do not practise forgiveness then God will withdraw his mercy.

Questions

1 a) How many times did Peter think a person should be forgiven?

b) How many times did Jesus say a person should be forgiven?

2 Retell the parable of the Unforgiving Servant.

3 Jesus preached and practised forgiveness.

a) Do you think his example is followed by people today?

b) Why do you think some people find it hard to forgive others?

The parable of the lost son

Luke 15:11-32

The parable of the lost son is one of the most popular parables Jesus told and has often been used in drama or rewritten in a modern version.

The parable illustrates that in the Kingdom of God forgiveness is possible, no matter how far someone has strayed from God.

Outline of the story

There was once a man who had two sons.

The younger son sold his part of the property, left home and wasted the money in reckless living. He spent everything he had. When a famine hit the country he was forced to take a job looking after pigs. He was so hungry he wanted to eat the bean pods which were used to feed the pigs. In Jewish tradition pigs are regarded as unclean. The younger son had sunk to the lowest depths – he was acting like a Gentile.

Finally he decided to return home, admit to his father that he had sinned and ask to be treated as one of his father's hired helpers. Obviously he did not expect to be forgiven.

The younger son was still a long way from home when his father saw him. His father's heart was filled with pity and he ran to greet him. Running would have been considered undignified for such a man. This shows the great joy he must have felt when he saw his son.

A party was organised for the son. He was given:
- the best robe;
- a ring: a symbol of authority, showing he was given back his rights as a son;
- shoes: a symbol of freedom.

The prize calf was killed for a celebration feast.

The elder son was very angry. He had worked for years for his father and had never received treatment like this. In this parable the elder son represents the Jewish leaders who thought they were the only people who should inherit God's kingdom and resented Jesus' idea that even sinners could be forgiven and enter the Kingdom.

His father told him to celebrate and be happy for it was as if his brother was dead and now was alive again.

Questions

1 *What did the younger son do with his share of the property?*
2 *The Torah outlined the punishment for rebelling against one's parents. What was it? (Deuteronomy Ch 21:18-21)*
3 *What did the younger son do when he had spent everything?*
4 *The younger son eventually "came to his senses". What does this mean in this situation?*
5 *How did the elder brother react to his younger brother's homecoming?*
6 *How was the behaviour of the elder brother like that of the Jewish leaders?*
7 *What does this parable teach about:*
    a) repentance?
    b) forgiveness?
    c) God?
8 *In your opinion, what lessons are there for today's parents and children in the parable of the lost son? Try to give some practical examples.*

Forgiveness in action

On 11 November 1987 an IRA bomb killed eleven people at a Remembrance Day service in Enniskillen. One of those killed was a 20 year old nurse, Marie Wilson. She died by her father's side. When her father, Gordon Wilson, was later interviewed he said that even though he had lost his daughter, he bore no grudge. He re-echoed Jesus' teaching in the Lord's Prayer about forgiveness and commented that he prayed for the bombers.

The father of the youngest victim of the Enniskillen massacre, 20-year-old Marie Wilson, has recalled how he lay trapped beneath the rubble, holding his dying daughter's hand.
"I bear no grudge or ill-will against anyone; I have prayed for the people who set the bomb," said Mr Gordon Wilson in a spirit of unprecedented charity after he had recalled the last words his daughter had spoken to him as they lay trapped under six feet of rubble:- "Daddy, I love you very much." *Impartial Reporter*

Activity

1 *In groups consider the following questions:*
a) Why do you think Gordon Wilson was able to forgive the bombers?
b) Are there some things which you would consider to be unforgivable?
c) How can the Christian Church help people in Northern Ireland who have suffered bereavement as a result of the Troubles?

2 *Look at newspapers and magazine problem pages for examples of broken relationships. Choose one situation and identify the people involved. Write a script of what might have been said when the situation came to a head and show how it could be resolved by forgiveness.*

Enniskillen War Memorial. It was also badly damaged in the bomb. It has been restored and a dove was added for each of the people who died.

Wealth & Poverty

How important is money to you? In a local survey of 14-16 year olds, 100% of them said money was important to them. The pie-chart below shows how they spend their money.

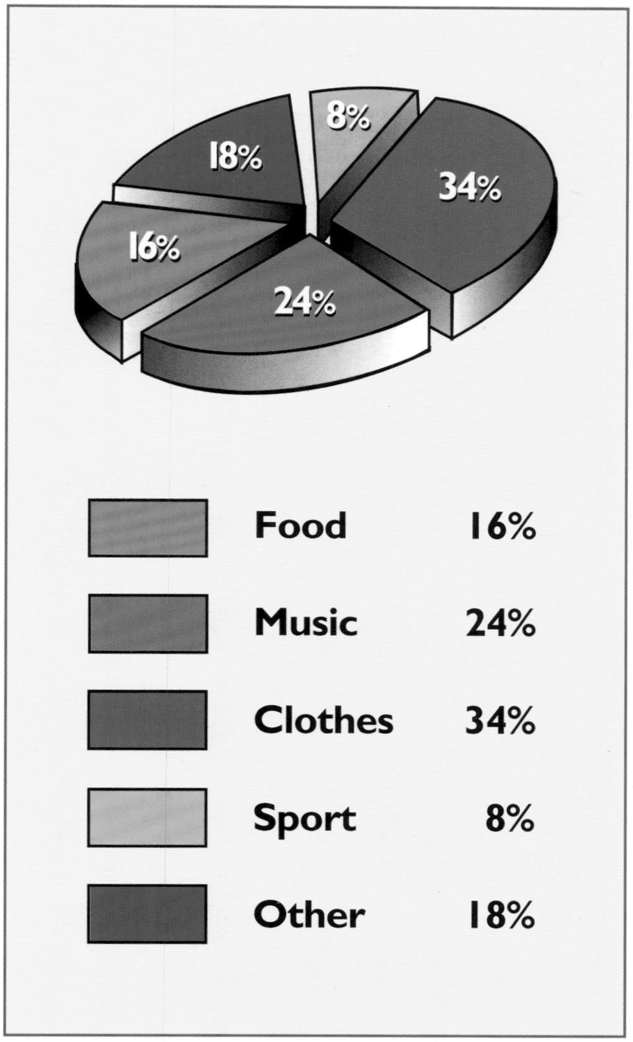

Activity

Draw your own pie-chart to show how you spend your money.

Teaching about charity

Matthew 6:1-4

The singer Bob Geldof on stage at the Live Aid concert which he organised in 1985 to raise money to relieve suffering caused by famine in Africa. Can you find out more about this concert and who took part? Why do you think Bob Geldof was so successful at raising money?

In Jesus' day religious duties involved charity, prayer and fasting. Jesus taught that those who carry out these duties to gain a good reputation get precisely that – but nothing more. "I assure you, they have already been paid in full." (v2) Jesus called such people **hypocrites**. In this case there were religious people who were giving money to charity, which is a kind and humble thing to do, yet they were proud and boastful about the way they did it. Instead Jesus taught that Christians should give to the needy in such a way that only God knows about it. Then they would be rewarded appropriately.

Look back at your pie-charts and see if anyone included giving to charity on theirs. The chances are that very few of you included it. However, Christians believe that giving to charity is very important, no matter how much money you have. There are many ways to give privately to charity. Look at the following list:

TV appeals
Sponsoring a child
Disaster Funds
Flag days

Can you think of any others?

Investigation

Your Task — **To investigate a Charity and the attitudes of people towards charities.**

Your Resources — **Interviews (Use the questions provided in the 'Questions' file.)**
Books etc. Try to find some of the items from the 'Books' file in your school library.
The internet. (Use the addresses in the 'websites' file.)

Your Results — **Try to present your findings in a creative and interesting way. Ask your teacher if you can use the black/white board, the overhead projector, a school computer or video camera.**

Questions (a)

You could use these questions to interview someone involved with a charity or when writing to a charity:

1. What is the aim or purpose to your charity and how did it begin?
2. How do you raise money?
3. How do you spend the money you raise?
4. Why do you think your charity is important?

Questions (b)

You could use these questions to make a survey for your class:

1. How often do you give money to charity?
2. What charities do you consider to be the most important?
3. Would you consider volunteering to do some charity work? What kind of work?
4. Do you think people will give more or less money to certain charities in the future? Why?

Books

'It's not Fair' published by Christian Aid, CAFOD and SCIAF
'Act Justly' (Drama sketches) published by Christian Aid and CAFOD
Charity magazines and brochures
Relevant newspaper articles

Websites

www.oneworld.org
www.cafod.org.uk
www.christian-aid.org.uk
www.habitat.org
www.oxfam.org.uk
www.tearfund.org.uk
www.oxfam.org.uk/coolplanet/index.html
www.trocaire.org/inde.html

Addresses

Christian Aid
48 Elmwood Ave.
Belfast BT9 6AZ

Northern Ireland Hospice
74 Somerton Road
Belfast BT15 3LH

Concern Worldwide
47 Frederick St.
Belfast BT1 2LW

Trocaire
50 King St.
Belfast BT1 6AD

Save the Children
17 Grove Lane
London SE5 8RD

One World Centre
4 Lower Crescent
Belfast BT7 1NR

Simon Community
57 Fitzroy Ave.
Belfast BT7 1HT

Oxfam
Most town centres have an Oxfam shop, or you could write to:
274 Banbury Rd.
Oxford OX2 7BR

The rich young man

Matthew 19:16-22

Discussion

In pairs discuss the following questions:
a) Would you want to win the lottery?
b) What would you do with the money if you won five million pounds?

The story of the rich young man illustrates that Jesus placed great importance on a person's attitude to money. The man wanted to know how to receive eternal life and Jesus told him to keep the Commandments. He told Jesus that he had obeyed all the Commandments, but he was aware that he needed something more. Jesus then told him the first step he could take in order to become 'perfect':

"... go and sell all you have and give the money to the poor, and you will have riches in heaven."
(v21)

The man knew that he would never be able to do this and he went away sad. His attachment to money was enough to keep him out of the Kingdom of Heaven. The story does not suggest that everyone who becomes a Christian must give up their possessions but that they must put God before material things.

The camel and the needle's eye

Matthew 19:23-30

Jesus then went on to tell his disciples:

"I assure you: it will be very hard for rich people to enter the Kingdom of Heaven. I repeat: it is much harder for a rich person to enter the Kingdom of God than for a camel to go through the eye of a needle."

The contrast between a camel, which was the largest animal found in Palestine, and the tiny hole of a needle makes it clear just how impossible it would be for the rich man to enter the Kingdom of Heaven.

The disciples were shocked to hear this teaching from Jesus because in Jewish culture riches were regarded as a blessing from God, a reward for good behaviour. If this was not the case then it seemed as if no-one could be saved.

Jesus' words in v26 show that the hope of salvation can only be achieved by God's initiative – in other words, salvation is a gift from God. The rich and the poor are all saved in the same way.

Peter, the spokesman of the disciples, pointed out that they had given up everything to follow Jesus. Jesus assured him that they would receive both entry into the Kingdom and great responsibility in the New Age (v28).

Furthermore, Jesus taught that all Christians who left their families or their jobs for his sake would be given eternal life. In that New Age, those who were weak, underprivileged, or marginalised on earth would be first, and those who had been greedy, unfair or who had abused their position of power would be last.

Questions

1 *Why did Jesus call some of the religious leaders 'hypocrites'?*

2 *Name two Jewish religious groups which were angered by Jesus' teaching on charity.*

3 *Why do many Christians believe it is important to donate money to charity?*

4 *a) Who asked "What good thing must I do to receive eternal life?"*
b) Name two things this man had to do to receive eternal life.
c) Why did the young man go away sad?

5 *What comparison did Jesus make to show how difficult it would be for a rich person to enter the Kingdom of Heaven?*

6 *Why would the disciples find it hard to accept the idea that riches could stand in the way of entry into the kingdom?*

7 *Explain what Jesus meant by saying "many who are first will be last and many who are last will be first."*

Activity

1 *In groups, discuss the following statements:*

"Money brings you food, but not appetite; medicine but not health; acquaintance but not friends; servants but not loyalty; days of joy but not peace or happiness" (Henrik Ibsen)

"Those who say money doesn't bring happiness are only jealous of those who are rich and satisfied. Of course money brings happiness."

Humility & Ambition

Who is the greatest?

Matthew 18:1-5

The disciples appear to have been arguing amongst themselves about who was the greatest. In New Testament times, as today, a lot of significance was attached to a person's status or place in society.

Jesus' answer showed that true greatness in the Kingdom of God is achieved by being humble. He used the example of a child, too young to have lost its innocence – a child does not try to make himself great. Unless Jesus' followers could become like such a child they would not even enter the Kingdom of Heaven.

True Christians should not put themselves first but should be concerned for everyone, even the weakest in the community.

Life after Death

Death has become a taboo subject in our society, something that people avoid speaking about in public. It wasn't always like this, but in recent history death has become a very private affair. Most people die in hospitals, are prepared for burial by undertakers and their funeral takes place in a church. In the past all of these things would have been part of home and family life.

Jesus, however, was not afraid to discuss the topic of death or the after-life.

The question about rising from death

Matthew 22:23-33

The Sadducees did not believe in life after death (**resurrection**). They followed the law of Moses (**Torah**) which did not specifically teach that there was life after death. So the Sadducees took any opportunity to debate with those who held such a belief.

In this incident the Sadducees were questioning Jesus about the law found in Deut. 25:5-6. This is known as the 'Levirate' law and it speaks of a man's duty to his brother's widow: a widow should remain part of the family and her dead husband's unmarried brother should take her as his wife.

The Sadducees asked Jesus a trick question about this (v24-28). Even though they did not believe in life after death, they asked Jesus whose wife a woman would be at the resurrection if she married seven brothers in her lifetime. They hoped Jesus' reply would show disrespect to the Law of Moses.

Jesus made two points:

1 There is no such thing as marriage in heaven.

2 There is a resurrection. Jesus quoted Exodus 3:6: "**I am** the God of Abraham, the God of Isaac and the God of Jacob." The use of the present tense highlights the fact that these men, although physically dead, are alive in heaven.

The final judgement (The parable of the sheep and the goats)

Matthew 25:31-46

In this parable the king (God) is the judge and the people of all the nations are brought before him to be judged according to their actions.

They are divided into two groups in the same way that a shepherd separates the sheep from the goats:

- righteous – on his right
- the others – on his left

The right side was often associated with blessing and the left side with a curse.

Jesus' teaching always emphasised the importance of doing God's will and not merely talking about it. This parable reinforces that point. The righteous are described as those who helped others when they were most in need. When they served others it was as if they were serving Jesus himself.

The unrighteous are those who did not help others when they had the opportunity. The parable reveals that people will be judged by their motives and attitudes.

In Palestine, sheep and goats are often mixed up together in one flock.

Discussion

a) If you believe in life after death, what do you think it will be like? Try to describe your mental picture to the rest of the class.

b) Look at sources A-C. Do you agree or disagree with the ideas about the afterlife contained in them?

c) Who do you think will go to Heaven?

Source A "Then I saw a new heaven and a new earth. The first heaven and the first earth disappeared, and the sea vanished. And I saw the Holy City, the new Jerusalem, coming down out of heaven from God, prepared and ready like a bride dressed to meet her husband. I heard a loud voice speaking from the throne: 'Now God's home is with mankind! He will live with them, and they shall be his people. God himself will be with them, and he will be their God. He will wipe away all tears from their eyes. There will be no more death, no more grief or crying or pain. The old things have disappeared.' "

Rev 21:1-4.

Source B *This is an extract from a real-life account of a near-death experience.*
I saw a pinpoint of Light in the distance. The black mass around me began to take on more of the shape of a tunnel, and I felt myself travelling through it at an even greater speed, rushing towards the light. ... As I approached it, I noticed the figure of a man standing in it, with the light radiating all around him. As I got closer the light became brilliant – brilliant beyond any description, far more brilliant than the sun and I knew that no earthly eyes in their natural state could look upon this light without being destroyed. Only spiritual eyes could endure it and appreciate it. ... I felt an utter explosion of love. ... the most unconditional love I have ever felt, and as I saw his arms open to receive me I went to him and received his complete embrace and said over and over, "I'm home. I'm home, I'm finally home." ... Gently, he opened his arms and let me stand back far enough to look into his eyes, and he said. "Your death was premature, it is not yet your time." ... Did this mean I would have to go back! I said to him, "No, I can never leave you now." He understood what I meant, and his love and acceptance for me never wavered. My thoughts raced on: "Is this Jesus, God, the being I feared all my life! He is nothing like what I had thought. He is filled with love."

Betty Brodsky

Source C *In the 14th century an Italian writer, Dante Alighieri, wrote about Hell in a poem called 'The Inferno'. The extracts below give some idea of what he thought it would be like:*
"Gross hailstones, water grey with filth, and snow come streaking down across the shadowed air; the earth as it receives that shower, stinks ...
That downpour makes the sinners howl like dogs; they use one of their sides to screen the other – those miserable wretches turn and turn."
In another place "flakes of fire showered down; their fall was slow - as snow descends on Alps when no wind blows ...
so did the never-ending heat descend; with this, the sand was kindled just as tinder on meeting flint with flame – doubling the pain."

The New Covenant

Matthew 5:21-48

A **covenant** is a promise or an agreement. In the Old Testament, God made a covenant with Abraham and the people of Israel. He would bless them and make them a great nation if they agreed to worship and obey only him. Unfortunately, the Israelites were not good at keeping their part of the agreement.

With the coming of Jesus, the promised Messiah, the old covenant was updated. Jesus recognised that outward observance of the Old Testament laws were not enough to please God – a person's attitudes and feelings were what mattered. In a section of the **Sermon on the Mount** (Matthew 5:21-48) Jesus gave six examples of Jewish teaching given by Moses and outlined his own interpretation of them.

1 Anger

Matthew 5:21-26

One of the Ten Commandments reads: "Do not commit murder, anyone who does will be brought to trial." Jesus' teaching highlighted that there is a deeper meaning in the commandment. Christians should not even want to harm someone. In other words, they should not be so angry with another person that their anger develops into hatred. Indeed any sort of anger or rage is forbidden as Jesus taught that such emotions are as bad as the action of murder itself.

Jesus also condemned 'name-calling'. A person who has contempt for others or who insults them is in danger of going to hell.

2 Adultery

Matthew 5:27-30

Another commandment states "Do not commit adultery." Again Jesus added a new meaning. Christians should not want to commit adultery. Jesus taught that sin begins in the heart because thought leads to action.

Christians believe Jesus is not denying natural human desire. Rather he meant that Christians should not put themselves in the situation where they would be likely to feel tempted to lust after someone else's partner. Therefore the 'right eye' (v29) represents the means by which desires enter the mind. Removing oneself from the temptation is preferable to going to hell.

3 Divorce

Matthew 5:31-32

At the time of Jesus there was an ongoing debate over divorce and the question of when a divorce might be permitted. There were two main schools of thought which interpreted the teaching in the Old Testament in different ways.

Rabbi Shammai taught that divorce was only possible in the case of infidelity (unfaithfulness). **Rabbi Hillel**, on the other hand, taught that a man could divorce his wife simply if he found something about her that he didn't like, but this could mean anything and often women were divorced for very minor offences. All a man had to do was give his wife a written notice of divorce.

In the Sermon on the Mount Jesus taught that divorce should only be allowed if a man's wife had committed adultery. Therefore, if a man divorced his wife for any reason other than unfaithfulness, in God's eyes the couple were still married. If either partner went on to remarry they would then be guilty of committing adultery.

to limit revenge. So if a man knocked out your tooth, you could knock out his tooth and nothing more. Jesus taught that all revenge was wrong. He urged his followers to "turn the other cheek" even if severely provoked. In practice this meant trying to repay evil with good.

6 Love for enemies

Matthew 5:43-48

Leviticus 19:18 taught the Jews to "love your neighbour as you love yourself." In practice many people felt this meant they should love fellow Jews and it didn't matter if they hated their enemies. By the time of Jesus this attitude had developed into an unwritten law (see v43) but the words, "and hate your enemies", were not quoted in the Old Testament.

Jesus taught that there is nothing extraordinary about loving your friends: "Even the pagans do that." (v47) It is part of human nature. He urged his followers to be different by asking them to "love your enemies and pray for those who persecute you." Jesus was describing *agapé* love which can be explained as a practical love which requires effort. It is based on a respect for all people.

4 Vows

Matthew 5:33-37

Jesus taught that vows were not necessary because a Christian should always speak the truth and to doubt each other's honesty would be an insult. Furthermore, a Christian should not make a vow using God's name as this shows a lack of respect.

5 Revenge

Matthew 5:38-42

In the Old Testament revenge was allowed. The law of retaliation said: "An eye for an eye and a tooth for a tooth." The purpose of this was

Discussion

"How you live is more important than what you believe." Do you agree? Give reasons for your opinion.

Martin Luther King attempted to put the teachings of Jesus in the Sermon on the Mount into practice in his own life. He led the Civil Rights campaign during the 1960s in America which tried to achieve equality for black Americans.

Although his protest brought him into confrontation with the authorities he always insisted that his followers acted in a non-violent way. They participated in forms of protest such as sit-ins or mass meetings which people couldn't ignore but which weren't violent.

Martin Luther King's turn-the-other-cheek policy represented the best way to make his point; to expose the brutality of his opponents and to create a positive, harmonious future.

"Love even for enemies is the key to the solution of the problems of our world – Jesus is not an impractical idealist; he is the practical realist."

"Darkness cannot drive out darkness; only light can do that. Hate cannot drive out hate; only love can do that. Hate multiplies hate, violence multiplies violence and toughness multiplies toughness ... so when Jesus says 'Love your enemies,' he is setting forth a profound and ultimately inescapable admonition."

('Strength to Love', Martin Luther King Hodder & Stoughton 1964.)

Questions

1 a) Which of the Ten Commandments did Jesus refer to in the New Covenant? (see Exodus chapter 20).
b) Complete the following table:

	Old Testament Law	New Covenant
ANGER		
ADULTERY		
DIVORCE		
VOWS		
REVENGE		
LOVE FOR ENEMIES		

2 Do you think Jesus' teaching on non-violence is a practical guide for Christian behaviour today?

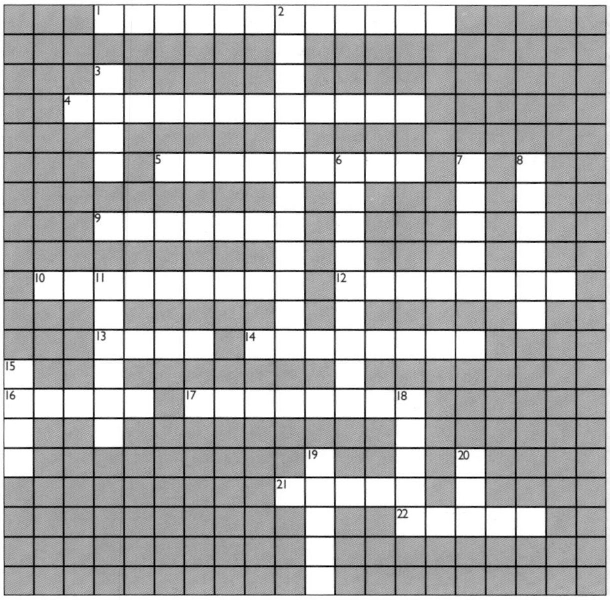

Teachings of Jesus crossword

Across
1. The Sadducees did not believe in this (12)
4. A central theme in all the Gospels (7,2,3)
5. Another name for the Lord's Prayer (3,6)
9. A common teaching method used by Jesus (7)
10. This is the seed in the parable of the sower (4,2,3)
12. An agreement or promise (8)
13. Killed for a feast (4)
14. Asking in prayer (8)
16. Leads to murder (5)
17. Construction workers (8)
21. Light does this (5)
22. The righteous (5)

Down
2. Alone eyed fee (anagram) (3,2,1,6)
3. A symbol of authority (4)
6. Someone who does not practice what they preach (9)
7. Peter said he would forgive his brother this number of times (5)
8. Even these people love their friends (6)
11. Considered a blessing from God in Jewish culture (6)
15. Flavours and preserves (4)
18. A symbol of freedom (5)
19. Jesus urged his followers to become like this one (5)
20. You lose one if you take one (3)

The Greatest Story Ever Told, United Artists

The Deeds of Jesus

The Gospel writers were keen to show that Jesus was not just a man of words but a man of action as well. They considered Jesus' deeds central to understanding the whole of his life because they:

- showed Jesus' compassion and love for people
- proved that what he said was true
- were evidence of his special relationship with God
- provided an example for Christ's followers to live by.

Miracles

Many of the deeds of Jesus which we will be looking at in this unit were **miracles**. Today there is much discussion over the nature of Jesus' miracles – were they actual supernatural events or did they just seem to be amazing when, in reality, they had a logical and scientific explanation?

The Gospel writers do not give detailed scientific accounts of the miracles because they were writing at a time when miracles were simply taken for granted. Their aim was not to prove that a particular event was a miracle but to highlight the amazing way in which God had worked through Jesus.

Discussion

Christians today don't always agree about what happened on the occasions when Jesus performed miracles. Look at the views below and decide which one is closest to your point of view:

"I'm suspicious about whether miracles were supernatural events. Surely these sorts of things were said to be done by all the great founders of religion. I'm sure there's a logical explanation to them."

"All miracles in the Bible were the work of God and shouldn't be doubted. If the Bible says Jesus turned water into wine then that is exactly what he did."

"Miracles can neither be believed blindly or simply rejected because they don't make scientific sense. They are significant because they show the greatness of Christ, which the Gospel writers express in colourful and creative language."

Jesus' Treatment of Women and the Poor

In Jesus' time men were regarded as being the superior sex and women had a low status in society. There were various rules about how females could behave in public and in many aspects of life they did not have equal rights: only boys were given the chance of an education at the synagogue; women worshipped separately from men and could not enter the inner courts of the Temple; in marriage a man could divorce his wife easily whereas a woman could not divorce her husband.

Jesus' treatment of women differed from the way the majority of men of his time treated them. He spoke to them frequently, accepted their help and spent time with them (Luke 10:38-42). He was not afraid of criticism from others for his actions and had several female followers, some of whom stayed with him at the cross, and it was to women that Jesus first appeared after the resurrection.

Jesus heals Simon's mother-in-law

Luke 4:38-40

While Jesus was in Capernaum on the Sabbath, Simon Peter's mother-in-law was ill so Jesus healed her. When the fever left her she began to wait on those present, indicating that she had made a full recovery. This was very significant because not only had Jesus taken time to heal a woman but he had performed this miracle on the Sabbath.

The Law stated that no work could be done on the Sabbath (Jeremiah 17:24). The religious leaders believed this was the case even if it involved helping the sick and needy.

After sunset (which marked the end of the Sabbath) those who had witnessed the miracle brought their friends who needed healing to Jesus. Demons left people and were silenced by Jesus because they recognised him as being the Messiah.

The Sabbath: *The Sabbath day began at 6 pm on Friday and lasted until 6 pm on Saturday. The word 'sabbath' comes from the Hebrew 'shabat' which means 'to cease'. All work stopped on that day. Even today in Israel you will find shops closed and limited transport on the Sabbath. Look up the following references to see why this day is kept so strictly:*

** Genesis 2:2*
** Exodus 20:11*
** Numbers 15:32-36*

Jesus at the home of Simon the Pharisee

Luke 7:36-50

On this occasion Jesus was having a meal at the home of Simon the Pharisee (not to be confused with Simon Peter, the disciple). While Jesus was there he was approached by a sinful woman (a prostitute) who washed his feet with her tears, dried them with her hair and anointed them with perfume. The woman's treatment of Jesus was very generous.

The woman's actions were all the more significant because Simon, the host, had not provided Jesus with water for his feet, as was the normal custom for guests who had been travelling along dusty roads. Simon's lack of hospitality is in contrast to the woman's generosity.

Simon inwardly criticised Jesus' acceptance of the woman's gestures. Jesus, sensing Simon's disapproval, told a parable.

One man owed a lot of money to a money-lender. Another man owed a small amount. The money lender cancelled both debts. Jesus asked: "Which one, then, will love him more?" The answer was obvious to Simon, "… the one who was forgiven more." Jesus then explained that this parable illustrated that the woman's actions stemmed from her appreciation that she had been forgiven. Jesus words to the woman, "Your sins are forgiven", caused those present to question his identity because they thought only God could do this. The woman, however, had shown great faith and was commended for it.

Jairus' daughter

Luke 8:40-42 & 49-56

Jesus had just returned from Gerasa when he was met by a crowd of people. Jairus, an official in the local synagogue, begged Jesus to cure his only daughter who was dying. On the way to Jairus' house Jesus took time to heal a woman who had suffered from severe bleeding for 12 years. As Jesus was speaking to this woman a messenger arrived from Jairus' house to tell them it was too late; the young girl had died. Jesus' comment in v50 emphasises the importance of faith in this miracle. He took Peter, John and James along with the child's mother and father into the house. The young girl was surrounded by people crying and mourning. They laughed when Jesus suggested the child was only sleeping, but Jesus took the girl by the hand and told her to get up. Everyone was astonished when she did so.

This miracle shows both the power Jesus had over death and the great love he had for women and children. Jesus wanted to give Jairus back his only daughter.

The woman who touched Jesus' cloak

Luke 8:43-48

This miracle forms part of the narrative of the raising of Jairus' daughter from the dead. The woman may have been suffering from haemophilia. In the eyes of the Jewish law, her condition made her ceremonially unclean, preventing her from joining in Jewish religious ceremonies and festivals. Her obvious embarrassment made it necessary for her to approach Jesus secretly (v44) and touch the edge of his cloak. This also showed her great faith which is the key to understanding this miracle. Jesus was aware of what was happening (v46) and that someone needed his help. The woman had faith in God to restore her health. When he commended her for her faith: "My daughter, your faith has made you well. Go in peace", he showed the deep regard he had for women. Clearly Jesus put them on an equal footing with men. He also wanted the woman to know that her faith played a part in making her well.

Jesus heals a crippled woman on the Sabbath

Luke 13:10-17

On this occasion Jesus was teaching in a synagogue when he saw a woman who was obviously suffering from an arthritic illness. Jesus later explained that the woman had been bound by Satan for eighteen years, suggesting that she had an evil spirit. Healing came as a result of Jesus' words: "Woman, you are free from your illness."

The synagogue official criticised Jesus because he had healed the woman on the Sabbath. Jesus replied that if an animal could be attended to on the Sabbath then surely a person needing help could be freed from an illness. By saying this, Jesus embarrassed the religious leaders and showed them that taking the law to extremes was not in the interests of helping people. The fact that Jesus was prepared to heal a woman on the Sabbath and risk criticism, showed how much he cared.

The widow's offering

Luke 21:1-4

This incident reflects Jesus' attitude towards both women and the poor. It took place at the Temple treasury which was found in the Court of Women (see p11 for a diagram of the Temple). Jesus compared the action of the poor widow, who gave all she had to live on, with the actions of the rich people who gave what they could spare from their riches. Christians understand from this that the sacrifice involved in giving is more important than the amount given.

Judaism today

In traditional Judaism women are seen as separate but equal to men. They have different roles and responsibilities to men, but they are considered no less important. An **Orthodox** (traditional) Jewish woman is not allowed to say the ritual prayers unless a man is present and in the synagogue they sit separately from men. Their views on divorce still prevent a woman from divorcing her husband.

In **Progressive Judaism** women are regarded as being equal to men. They can be part of the leadership of the synagogue – it is not unusual for a woman to be a rabbi (teacher) and women can begin divorce proceedings.

Try to find out more by looking at these websites:
http:www.jewfaq.org/index.htm
http:www.clickonjudaism.com

This is Rabbi Julia Neuberger. She became Chancellor of the University of Ulster in 1993

Questions

1. ***What was wrong with Simon's mother-in-law and how did Jesus heal her?***
2. ***When Jesus was having dinner at the house of Simon the Pharisee what did a woman do to cause offence to those gathered?***
3. ***Outline the parable Jesus told about a money lender.***
4. ***Complete Jesus words: "But whoever has been forgiven little . . ."***
5. ***a) Who was Jairus and what did he ask Jesus to do?***
   b) Describe what happened on the way to Jairus' house.
   c) Who went with Jesus into the house?
   d) What happened when Jesus spoke to the child?
6. ***a) Who did Jesus heal when he was teaching in a synagogue on the Sabbath?***
   b) Explain why the official of the synagogue became angry at this.
   c) Jesus' answer made his enemies feel ashamed of themselves. What did he say?
7. ***a) Where did the widow make her offering and how much did she give?***
   b) Why did Jesus suggest that she had given more than the rich men?
   c) What can Christians learn from her?

Discussion

1. ***What can Christians learn from Jesus' attitude to women?***
2. ***The Church of Ireland, Presbyterian, and Methodist churches all have women ministers. Do you think that all churches should be more open to allowing women to be leaders?***
3. ***In your opinion, is it okay to joke about "a woman's place being in the home"? Is it harmless fun or does it encourage discrimination?***
4. ***Prepare a speech for a class debate on the following:***

   "Men and women are equal but they should accept that they have different roles in the Christian Church."

Jesus' Treatment of Foreigners

The Jews considered themselves to be God's chosen people. As a result, foreigners were considered to be outcasts. There were two groups of foreigners who are mentioned in the Gospels:

1 **The Romans**: In 63 BC the Romans entered Jerusalem and conquered Palestine. As an occupying army, the Romans were hated, although the authorities did allow local kings to rule the provinces.

2 **The Samaritans**: In 721 BC some Assyrians had settled in Palestine and intermarried with the local Jews. Their descendants were called Samaritans. The Jews hated them and despised their religion because they were a mixed race. At the time of Jesus there was an on-going historical struggle between the Jews and Samaritans.

Jesus heals a Roman officer's servant

Luke 7:1-10

In this miracle Jesus demonstrated that the Kingdom of God is open to everyone, both Jews and Gentiles. The Roman officer was a Gentile but he was sympathetic to Judaism. He might have been a **god-fearer** (someone who was interested in the Jewish religion but had not become a full Jew).

The Roman officer was obviously a kind man for he cared about the health of his servant. Usually in the Roman world slaves had no rights and no help if they fell ill. He sent some Jewish elders to ask Jesus for help because his servant was ill. The Roman officer would have been used to giving orders but he recognised that Jesus had a much greater authority which came from God. Jesus praised him for his faith: ". . . I have never found faith like this, not even in Israel" (v9). The healing of the servant was made possible by the faith of this Roman officer. Notice that Jesus met neither the Roman officer nor his servant and performed the miracle at a distance.

Faith and miracles

On all the occasions when Jesus performed a miracle he did it for a specific purpose. He never used it to show off and he never did it to satisfy people's curiosity but he performed miracles for those who showed faith in him. However, it is important to note that he did not perform the miracle in order to bring a person to faith but the miracles were always a result of people's faith. Faith came first, then the miracle.

Discussion

1 Read sources A and B below.

In your opinion, are they examples of miracles? Give reasons.

2 Do you think miracles still happen today?

3 "If people had greater faith, there would be more miracles." What do you think?

Faith healing

A. Australian man cured of cancer

"Lucas came to a Friday night Healing Meeting very weak and ill. He had just been diagnosed as having cancer of the liver, pancreas and prostate gland. Doctors told him that his life expectancy was six weeks. He also had poisoned blood because he was a Pest Controller and handled a

lot of poisonous sprays. The Spirits of Cancer, Tumour and Malignancy were bound and cast out, inherited spirits of cancer were also cast out and the cells of cancer commanded to die from the roots. Then we prayed for re-creation of all damaged cells in the liver, pancreas and prostate glands. We also commanded the poison to be cleansed from his blood. Lucas felt the anointing of God that night and began to feel much better and stronger and the colour returned to his face. We prayed for him again in the next few meetings and were amazed at how well he seemed. Three weeks later he had to return to the Doctor to discuss the possibility of surgery. When the Doctor examined him they could find no trace of cancer."

B. Lourdes

Lourdes is a small town in the south west of France situated at the foot of the Pyrenees. However, every year five million visitors visit Lourdes to make a pilgrimage to the place where a young girl named Bernadette received visions of the Virgin Mary. Many of the pilgrims who go to Lourdes are sick or disabled because it is known as a place of special healing. One man recently healed there was Mr Jean-Pierre Bély. Here is part of an official report written by a Doctor in Lourdes.

"In 1972 Mr Bély was diagnosed with Multiple Sclerosis. From 1984 he required the use of a walking stick and he stopped working. By 1986 it was impossible for him to stand and he was confined to a wheelchair.

During a pilgrimage to the Sanctuary of Lourdes, Mr Bély regained completely his normal functions. On 9th October 1987, he received the Sacrament of the Sick in a morning mass and by midday found himself sitting on the side of his bed, and was surprised to move his arms and feel contact against his skin.

During the night that followed he woke up suddenly and had the surprise of being able to walk for the first time since 1984. Within 24 hours he had made a complete recovery.

After regular checks from 1987 to 1999 it is now possible to conclude that Mr Bély's cure is an inexplicable fact to all the knowledge of science."

Dr Patrick Thellier

The parable of the Good Samaritan

Luke 10:25-37

The parable of the Good Samaritan is one of the best-known parables told by Jesus. It was told as part of a conversation Jesus had with a teacher of the law who was trying to trap him into saying something which would be blasphemous. He asked Jesus a question about receiving eternal life. The Jews believed that only those belonging to God's chosen people, either by birth or conversion, and who kept the Law of Moses, would have eternal life. When Jesus asked him what the Scriptures said, he chose two commandments (see Deuteronomy 6:5 and Leviticus 19:18) :

(i) to love God with all your heart;
(ii) to love your neighbour as yourself.

Jesus approved of this interpretation of the law.

In the Old Testament the second of these commandments applied to loving foreigners as well but by the time of Jesus the law had become restricted to loving Jews alone. The teacher of the law, wanting to justify himself, went on to ask Jesus, "Who is my neighbour?" (v29) This question could have started an argument about whether Romans or outcasts were counted as being neighbours. Jesus answered his question by telling him the parable of the Good Samaritan.

The scene is set on the lonely stretch of road between Jerusalem and Jericho. The distance between them is 15 miles, a day's walk. It was notorious for muggings and attacks. In this story, a man was on his way to Jericho when he was beaten, robbed and left half dead. Both a priest and a Levite passed by without helping the man. They were religious figures who kept closely to the Jewish law. Thinking he was dead they were probably reluctant to touch the man for fear of being declared ritually unclean and unable to do their jobs in the Temple (see Numbers 19:11). This would be more important to them than helping someone in need.

However, when a Samaritan came along, he stopped and took pity on the injured man. He was clearly a rich man and he too would have been a target for robbers. Yet he put himself out and acted like a true neighbour.

When Jesus had finished telling the parable he asked a question: "Which one of these three acted like a neighbour towards the man attacked by robbers?"

The teacher of the law answered "The one who was kind to him." He could not even bring himself to say the word "Samaritan".

You have probably heard this parable more than once before. Many of you will also have read modern versions of the story or perhaps acted out the story in a drama. The lessons to be learned from it are still relevant for Christians today. The Samaritan's actions teach respect for all people regardless of religion, colour or social standing.

Questions

1. ***In Luke chapter 7 what was wrong with the Roman Officer's servant?***
2. ***a) How is the Roman officer described as being a good man?***
   b) What name was given to Gentiles who were sympathetic to Judaism?
3. ***What did the Roman officer's friend say to Jesus?***
4. ***What did Jesus say about the faith of the Roman officer?***
5. ***Explain why the Jews disliked the Samaritans.***
6. ***In Luke chapter 10, why was Jesus asked "What must I do to receive eternal life?"***
7. ***Retell the story of the Good Samaritan.***
8. ***Jesus gave guidelines on how to treat others on several occasions. Summarise his teaching using the following references:***
   - ***Matthew 25:40***
   - ***Matthew 22:39***
   - ***1 John 3:17-18***

Discussion

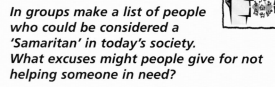

In groups make a list of people who could be considered a 'Samaritan' in today's society.
What excuses might people give for not helping someone in need?

Jesus' Treatment of Sinners

Jesus and Zacchaeus

Luke 19:1-10

As a tax collector, Zacchaeus was unpopular for two reasons. Firstly, he worked for the Romans who imposed the taxes on the people and were an occupying force in the country. Secondly, he cheated people out of money by over-charging them and keeping the extra money for himself. Jesus must have met Zacchaeus before as he was able to call him by name when he asked to go to his house. It was the custom for rabbis (teachers) to be given overnight accommodation by their listeners. The surprising thing was that Jesus chose Zacchaeus. Most people disapproved of this and started grumbling, showing the extent to which Zacchaeus was despised. Many of them would have considered themselves more worthy to have Jesus as a guest in their home.

Clearly Zacchaeus was touched by Jesus' acceptance of him for he publicly confessed his past black record and offered to do two things:

- give half his belongings to the poor;
- repay those he had cheated four times as much (see 2 Samuel 12:6).

Jesus' words in v9-10 show that Zacchaeus was now restored to his place in the community:
"Salvation has come to this house today, for this man, also, is a descendant of Abraham. The Son of Man came to seek and to save the lost."

Christians today believe they can learn from Jesus' example on this occasion. Instead of ignoring people or judging them because of their lifestyles, they believe it is important to go out of their way to be friendly, caring and help others to feel worthwhile.

Questions

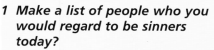

*1 **Why were tax collectors despised by the ordinary people?***
*2 **What did Jesus say to Zacchaeus when he looked up and saw him in the tree?***
*3 **Why did the people disapprove of this?***
*4 **What two things did Zacchaeus offer to do to make up for his past sins?***
*5 **Look up 2 Samuel 12:6. What relevance does this have to Zacchaeus' action?***
*6 **Why do you think Jesus was friendly to people like Zacchaeus?***

Discussion

*1 **Make a list of people who you would regard to be sinners today?***
*2 **Look at the following newspaper article:***

> **MINISTER'S SCORN!**
>
> *Minister tells congregation to ignore a church member who admitted to having an affair.*
>
> Yesterday, the Rev S Kennedy told his congregation to "have nothing to do with" Miss R Dillon, 21, who is having an affair with a married man.

a) What do you think Jesus would have done? Refer to teaching on the Sermon on the Mount (Unit 2) as well as taking into account Jesus' attitude to sinners.
b) What do you think of the minister's attitude? Refer to different points of view in your answer.
*3 **What can Christians learn from the way Jesus treated sinners such as Zacchaeus?***

Jesus' Treatment of Outcasts

At the time of Jesus there were several groups who were considered to be undesirable and were not allowed to take part in normal society. **Lepers**, for example, were considered **unclean** because of their disease. Their condition made it impossible for them to earn a living so many lepers found themselves destitute.

In Jesus' time leprosy was considered to be a punishment from God. People were afraid of catching the disease so lepers were isolated from the rest of society and forced to live in leper colonies.

Jesus heals a man with a dreaded skin disease

Luke 5:12-14

At the time of Jesus there were various skin diseases, not all of which were leprosy, but which made a person a social outcast. Strict instructions were given in the Old Testament to help prevent the spread of such diseases (see Leviticus 13:45-46).

On this occasion Jesus showed great compassion because he not only healed the man but he touched him. Many people would have been amazed at this because they believed that contact with the unclean made you unclean. Jesus was not comfortable with the fact that the law isolated someone from society because they had been pronounced unclean.

The man showed great faith when he said to Jesus "Sir, if you want to, you can make me clean."

Jesus advised the man to go and show himself to the priest for examination. Only the priest had the authority to declare a person clean again. As had happened before, Jesus told him not to tell anyone else about the miracle.

Jesus heals ten men

Luke 17:11-19

The ten men who needed healing were Jews and Samaritans. They too were suffering from "a dreaded skin disease". The men stood at a distance and shouted to attract Jesus' attention because anyone suffering from a skin disease had to keep away from everyone else. They called Jesus 'Master' because they had obviously heard of his ability to heal and they wanted to show him respect. Jesus told them to go to the priests for examination for he knew that the Law required this. On this occasion the only one who came back to thank Jesus for healing him was a Samaritan. As a Samaritan and a leper he would have been regarded as being even more separated from God than the other nine. Jesus recognised the man as being a foreigner and commended him for his faith.

Jesus heals a blind beggar

Luke 18:35-43

Jesus was making his journey to Jerusalem when he came near to Jericho. A blind beggar sitting by the road called out to him, asking for healing. The blind man addressed Jesus as 'Son of David', showing that he recognised he was the Messiah. Faith again played a great part in this miracle and Jesus commended him for it. Having received his sight, the man followed Jesus, meaning that he became a disciple. Note that on this occasion Jesus did not ask the man to keep quiet about what had happened. Jesus knew that he was approaching the end of his own life.

Questions

1 ***What did Jesus do when a leper said to him, "Sir, if you want to, you can make me clean"?***
2 ***When Jesus met the ten lepers, what did they shout out to him?***
3 ***Who came back to thank Jesus and why was this significant?***
5 ***Leprosy sufferers were outcasts in the time of Jesus. Who do you think are outcasts today?***
6 ***Who called Jesus 'Son of David' and what did this title mean?***
7 ***Explain how the blind man in Luke 18 showed his faith.***
9 ***What do you think Christians can learn from Jesus' attitude to the sick and disabled?***

Discussion

Read the interview with Sam Smith of the Leprosy Mission on the next page. How does the work of the Leprosy Mission reflect Jesus' attitude to outcasts?

Find out more:
The Leprosy Mission
(Northern Ireland)
4 Ulsterville Avenue
BELFAST
N Ireland
BT9 7AQ
Telephone: 01232 381937

The Leprosy Mission

Interview with Sam Smith, *Development Officer, Leprosy Mission, Northern Ireland.*

What is leprosy?

Leprosy is a disease caused by a bacillus which thrives in the cooler nerves of the body. These nerves normally serve the hands, feet, and face. When these nerves become damaged they can no longer register pain. This is very dangerous because loss of feeling can lead to injuries through burns to hands or sharp stones on unprotected feet. Faces can also be affected as sufferers may be unable to blink with dust and infection damaging the eyes. As well as the physical symptoms, there is much superstition and stigma associated with leprosy. The Leprosy Mission aims to teach the truth about leprosy.

Who is affected by leprosy?

Leprosy affects millions of people, 90% of whom live in the developing world. It is not hereditary and is difficult to catch; it cannot be caught by a handshake or sharing food with someone who has the disease. In fact over 95% of the world's population is naturally immune but we still see 600,000 new cases every year, that is, one new case every minute of the day.

What is the Leprosy Mission?

The Leprosy Mission is a Christian medical mission caring for people who suffer from leprosy. It was founded in 1874 by an Irishman called Wellesley Bailey. He said: "I felt, if ever there was a Christ-like work in this world it was to go among these poor sufferers and bring them the consolation of the Gospel."

Can leprosy be cured?

Leprosy can be cured using Multidrug Therapy (MDT). As the majority of leprosy sufferers are non-infectious they can be cured in 6-12 months, while infectious patients using MDT can be rendered non-infectious in 48 hours.

What do you see as the aim of the Leprosy Mission as we enter the Millennium?

Telling people of Jesus.
Lessening ignorance about leprosy.
Making MDT available to all leprosy sufferers.

Dr Johannes Schäfer and a Sudanese leprosy worker examining children during The Leprosy Mission team visit to Darfur in March 1996.

Jesus' Treatment of Religious Leaders

Jesus' attitudes were very different to those of the religious authorities. The crowds flocked to Jesus to hear his teaching and experience healing. The Jewish leaders found Jesus' teaching offensive and often tried to trap him by asking difficult questions. There was increasing conflict between them. Jesus was popular with the ordinary people so the religious authorities took every opportunity to try to show him up in public or prove him wrong.

Jesus heals a sick man

Luke 14:1-6

This is another miracle concerned with the issue of healing on the Sabbath (see also Luke 4:38-40 and Luke 13:10-17). On this occasion, as before, Jesus claimed the right to heal on the Sabbath if it involved helping someone in need.

Jesus had been invited for a meal at the home of one of the leading Pharisees when he saw a sick man who had dropsy. This painful condition is caused by liquid in the body's tissue, resulting in swelling. Knowing the Pharisees were watching him Jesus asked: "Does our Law allow healing on the Sabbath or not?" (v3) They said nothing and after healing the man Jesus commented:

" If any one of you had a son or an ox that happened to fall into a well on the Sabbath, would you not pull them out at once on the Sabbath itself?" (v5)

The Pharisees had no answer to this.

Humility and hospitality

Luke 14:7-14

As they were gathering for the meal Jesus noticed how some of the guests were choosing the best seats for themselves. So Jesus told them a parable about how to behave when invited to someone's house. He used a wedding feast as an example.

Jesus suggested that people should not automatically sit in the best seats because there might be someone more important invited and it would be embarrassing to be moved. Instead people should choose the lowest seat, for then there is a good chance of being moved to a better one which would bring them great honour in the presence of the other guests.

Jesus was getting at the religious leaders by telling this parable. The Pharisees in particular loved to be praised and given places of honour. Jesus knew their feelings of greatness would be short lived:

"For all those who make themselves great will be humbled, and those who humble themselves will be made great."

(v11)

Jesus then spoke to the host of the meal and suggested to him that real blessing could be found by inviting the poor, the crippled, the lame and the blind to a feast.

To illustrate his point Jesus went on to tell another parable. This parable is also an example of an allegory (see page 33).

The parable of the great feast

Luke 14:15-24

A man was giving a feast and invited many people. But when the time came for the feast the guests made excuses not to go (v18-20). So the host sent his servant to the streets of the town to invite others to take their places at the feast. These guests included the poor, the crippled, the blind and the lame. When there was still room left at the feast the servant was sent to the countryside to find more guests. The host was determined that none of the original guests would taste his dinner.

Symbolism of this allegory		
Feast	=	Kingdom of God
Original guests	=	The Jewish leaders who rejected the invitation to enter the Kingdom of God
Second guests	=	Outcasts or Jewish sinners
Third guests	=	Gentiles

This parable shows that the Kingdom of God is open to both Jew and Gentile alike.

The question about Jesus' authority

Luke 20:1-8

Jesus was in the Temple preaching when the chief priests, teachers of the law and the elders challenged his authority (v2):

"Tell us, what right have you to do these things? Who gave you this right?"

They were probably referring to Jesus' action of driving the traders from the Temple (Luke 19:45-46). Whatever Jesus said in reply would have aggravated the religious leaders and given them an excuse to harm him. If he had said God gave him the authority then they would have accused him of blasphemy. If he had said he was acting under his own authority they would have laughed at him.

Instead of answering them directly, Jesus asked them a question (v4):

"Did John's right to baptise come from God or from human beings?"

They, too, now found themselves in an awkward position. If they had said that John got his authority from God then the people would wonder why they did not believe him. If they had said he got his authority from himself then the crowd would be furious and might cause a riot for they were convinced that John was a prophet. In the end they said they didn't know.

The parable of the tenants in the vineyard

Luke 20:9-19

After Jesus' authority had been questioned by the religious leaders he told a parable. This parable is another example of an allegory.

In Palestine it was not unusual for foreigners to own land. This land was rented out to tenants who worked on it. If an owner died and left no-one to inherit the property, then the tenants had the chance to purchase the land.

This parable is an **allegory** because the events and characters are all symbolic:

owner	=	**God**
servants	=	**Old Testament prophets**
son	=	**Jesus**
tenants	=	**Jewish religious leaders**
new tenants (others)	=	**Gentiles**

Note that the son is killed outside the vineyard. This is symbolic of Jesus' death which took place outside the city of Jerusalem.

Jesus finished the parable by saying:

"The stone which the builders rejected as worthless turned out to be the most important of all." (v17)

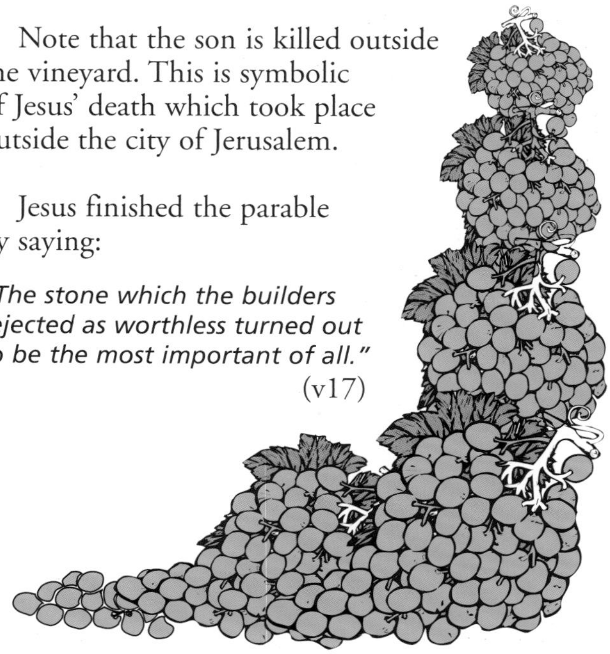

Jesus saw himself as the rejected stone which was in fact the stone which holds the whole structure together. He was thrown aside at his crucifixion by the Jewish religious leaders but he would come back to take his rightful place after the resurrection. As the most important stone, Christians believe that Jesus is the foundation on which their belief should rest.

The parable of the Tenants in the Vineyard made the Jewish religious leaders angry because they believed themselves to be God's chosen people. The parable suggested that they could be rejected. The Kingdom would be taken from them and given to someone else – the outcasts and the Gentiles.

Activity

Decipher the anagrams below.
The words can all be found in this unit.
Write a sentence which explains the meaning of each word in terms of the deeds of Jesus.

CAMEL SIR
GRIEF SNORE
A SILVER MINUS
A RAIN MAST
A USA CZECH
ROSE PLY
IDEAL OGRE RULE SIS
ROYAL GEL
ASHER PIE
SCOUT SAT

Questions

1 a) On which day of the week did Jesus go to eat a meal at the home of a leading Pharisee?
b) Why did Jesus ask whether the Law allowed healing on the Sabbath?
c) When Jesus healed the man, what question did he then put to the Pharisees and how did they respond?
d) This was not the first time Jesus was criticised for healing on the Sabbath. Why do you think people were so offended?

2 a) What were some people doing at this meal regarding the seating arrangements?
b) Why did Jesus advise people not to pick out the best seats for themselves?
c) Explain why this parable caused offence to those religious leaders present.
d) What did one guest say which led to Jesus telling the parable of the great feast?

3 a) In the parable what happened when it was time for the feast?
b) What did the master do as a result of his anger?
c) Explain how the parable of the great feast is an example of universalism.

'Ben Hur, MGM, 1959

Jesus' Death, Resurrection & Ascension

Death brings feelings of sadness, loss, distress, heartache and grief. Those closest to Jesus were devastated by his death, but Christians now look back on it as something to celebrate because he came to life again. They believe that through his death and resurrection Jesus defeated evil and made it possible for all people to become members of the Kingdom of God.

In this unit we will look at the events surrounding the death, resurrection and ascension of Jesus and the meaning these events still have for Christians today.

Jesus in Jerusalem

The destruction of the Temple and the end times

Matthew 24:1-14

If you look back at page 11 you will see what the Temple in Jerusalem would have looked like. At the time of Jesus the Temple was rebuilt by Herod the Great, but this magnificent building did not stand long – in AD 70 it was destroyed by the Romans. At the beginning of Matthew chapter 24, Jesus predicted the destruction of the Temple, and in reply his disciples asked him two questions:

1 When will the Temple be destroyed?

2 What will happen to show that the end of the world is near?

Jesus did not give a direct answer to the first question but he spoke about what will happen in the end times. There will be false Messiahs, battles, wars, natural disasters, persecution, evil and many people will deny their faith – Jesus called these the birth pangs of the New Age. He also said there would be some positive aspects to the end times. The good news will be preached throughout the world and those Christians who hold out to the end, despite the persecution, will be saved.

Jesus' death, resurrection and ascension are the most important events of his life. Christians remember and celebrate these events during Easter. The climax of the festival of Easter is **Holy Week**, the week leading up to Jesus' death and resurrection. You can see the days of Holy Week in the table below. Copy the table into your notebook and as you go through this unit, record the main events which happened on each day.

DAY	*EVENTS*	*REFERENCE*
Palm Sunday	Jesus rides into Jerusalem	Matthew 21: 1-11
Fig Monday	Jesus goes to the Temple	Matthew 21: 12-17
Holy Tuesday		
Wednesday		
Maundy Thursday		
Good Friday		
Holy Saturday		
Easter Day		

It is probable that by the time Matthew was writing he thought that Jesus' return (**parousia**) was approaching. The Church was facing persecution and the Temple may already have been destroyed in the battles between the Romans and the Jews. He was therefore stressing to his readers in the early church the importance of being true to their faith and continuing to spread the message about the Kingdom of God. In the same way Christians today believe that they too should be ready for Christ's return.

Jesus eats the Passover Meal with his disciples.

Matthew 26:17-25

The Passover meal is still celebrated every year by Jews today. It is a celebration of the Exodus, the night when the Israelites escaped from Egypt where they had been slaves. Jesus had obviously made some preparations for the night of his last Passover and on the appropriate day he sent his disciples to make sure that everything was ready. He may have kept the arrangements a secret because he knew he had a traitor among his followers.

The members of this modern Jewish family are praying together before eating their Seder meal.

The Passover or Seder meal which Jesus had would probably have consisted of:

- An opening prayer and blessing of the cup.
- Herbs dipped in salt water.
- Unleavened bread broken.
- The story of Passover told, then the second cup.
- The climax was the festive meal of roast lamb, then the third cup.

Some Biblical scholars suggest that the day on which Jesus had this Passover meal may not have been the official date for the festival but the calendar was not observed strictly by everyone at this time.

During the meal Jesus dramatically announced that he would be betrayed by someone sitting at the table who shared his bowl. All the disciples wondered if they had somehow done something to betray Jesus and Judas asked "Surely not me?", but the identity of the traitor was kept secret as they had all dipped their bread in a common dish.

This picture of The Last Supper was painted in 1955 by the Spanish artist, Salvador Dali (1904-1993). It is a very unusual interpretation. Do you like it? Talk about it in class. Who do you think is the figure with outstretched arms at the top of the picture? Why do you think the artist gave one of the disciples a yellow cloak? Many artists painted The Last Supper because it was such an important event – see if you can find other paintings of it. There is a very famous one by Leonardo da Vinci.

The Lord's Supper

Matthew 26:26-30

As we have already seen, this was a very important night for Jesus, but the activities which took place in that small room have become a central focus of the Christian Church for the past 2000 years. Christians today still remember the night when Jesus had his last supper by repeating the actions of eating bread and drinking wine. This ceremony, the **Eucharist**, is given different labels by different churches – for example, Mass, The Lord's Supper, Holy Communion and the Breaking of Bread.

Jesus explained that the bread was his body and the wine was his blood, which sealed God's covenant (see page 47). As part of the Old Covenant, Jews received God's blessing and forgiveness by making sacrifices at the Temple which showed their obedience and commitment to God.

At the Last Supper, Christians believe that a New Covenant was predicted, an agreement between God and all people. Jesus showed symbolically that at his death he would be the final sacrifice which would enable all people to receive God's blessing and forgiveness. This is what is meant by the phrase (v28):

"This is my blood which seals God's covenant, my blood poured out for many for the forgiveness of sins."

In verse 29 Jesus referred to the New Age, after death, when they would meet again.

In the **Roman Catholic Church** the Eucharist is celebrated in **the Mass**. They believe that the bread and wine change in substance to become the body and blood of Christ; so Christ becomes present in them. This is called **transubstantiation**.

In most Protestant churches, like the **Baptist Church,** communion is regarded as a memorial of Christ's death. They believe that the bread and wine do not change at all, instead they are symbols of what Christ has done. Communion means 'sharing' and these Christians are sharing together in the communion of Christ.

Jesus predicts Peter's denial

Matthew 26:31-35

In this passage Jesus makes three predictions:

1 His followers will be scattered after his death.
2 He will rise again.
3 Peter will deny him three times.

Although the second prediction seems to be the most amazing, his disciples do not seem to register its significance. Peter confidently shrugs off the suggestion that he could be unfaithful and says that he will not deny Jesus.

Questions

1 ***What is the week of Jesus' life before his crucifixion called?***
2 ***a) Where was Jesus when he spoke of the end of the world?***
b) According to Jesus' predictions what are the signs of the end times?
c) What did Jesus say about the person who holds onto their faith?
3 ***a) What were Jesus and his disciples celebrating at the Passover meal?***
b) In your own words explain what Jesus meant by saying: "This is my blood which seals God's covenant, my blood poured out for many for the forgiveness of sins"?
c) Explain how one Christian denomination today celebrates Christ's death.
4 ***a) What did Jesus say the disciples would all do before the night was over?***
b) What was Peter's response to the suggestion that he might deny Christ?

Arrest & Trials

Jesus prays in Gethsemane

Matthew 26:36-46

All the disciples made their way to the Garden of Gethsemane which was an olive tree plantation. Peter, James and John who had been with Jesus at the Transfiguration, his moment of glory, now went further into the garden to be with him in his time of suffering. The disciples must have been aware that something momentous was about to happen, yet they were unable to stay awake while Jesus agonised in prayer. On the one hand, he wanted to escape from the inevitable suffering which lay ahead. Yet, on the other hand, he wanted to do God's will, even if that meant torture and death. In Luke's Gospel it says that Jesus was in such anguish that "his sweat was like drops of blood falling to the ground" (Luke 22:44).

Jesus craved companionship in those dark moments and asked his disciples three times to stay awake, but they kept falling asleep so he had to cope with the mental suffering on his own. Christians believe that when they suffer things like illness, bereavement, injustice or simply being let down, they can pray to Jesus and he will understand because he has experienced such suffering himself. They also see Christ as giving an example of how to cope with problems. When he was in the Garden of Gethsemane, he prayed "Yet not what I want but what you want" and he handed his problems over to God.

This is part of the Garden of Gesthemane just outside Jerusalem.

Discussion

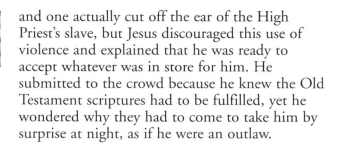

1. *Jesus prayed in his time of crisis in Gethsemane. In what circumstances do people today normally pray?*
2. *Do you think Jesus benefited from praying to God on this occasion?*
3. *In the film Shadowlands, CS Lewis, a Christian writer, says: "I don't pray because God answers prayer. I pray because I can't help myself. I pray because I am helpless, I pray because the need flows out of me all the time, waking and sleeping. It doesn't change God, it changes me."*
   Do you think prayer is important even if God doesn't seem to answer?

The arrest of Jesus

Matthew 26:47-56

Judas arrived with the Chief Priests, elders and an armed crowd to arrest Jesus. As it was dark it was necessary to have a clear sign to identify Jesus, so Judas kissed him on the cheek – a common greeting in that culture.

In a panic, Jesus' disciples tried to defend him and one actually cut off the ear of the High Priest's slave, but Jesus discouraged this use of violence and explained that he was ready to accept whatever was in store for him. He submitted to the crowd because he knew the Old Testament scriptures had to be fulfilled, yet he wondered why they had to come to take him by surprise at night, as if he were an outlaw.

Notice that his disciples were so shocked and petrified by what had happened that they ran away.

Jesus before the Council

Matthew 26:57-68

The **Sanhedrin** was the Jewish ruling council made up of Pharisees and Sadducees (see page 13). The head of the council was the **High Priest**, who at the time of Jesus was **Caiaphas**.

The council had power to govern the affairs of the Jewish population in Palestine and they had most of the powers of a normal court. One thing they could not do, however, was to carry out the death penalty. They could *sentence* someone to death but they could not actually carry it out. Only the Romans could do that.

This is a film maker's idea of one of Jesus' trials. It is from the film King of Kings, released in 1961.

The charge on which Jesus was brought before the court was one of **blasphemy** – speaking in an offensive way about God. It seems that the Jewish leaders did not care about giving Jesus a fair trial as it states that they were happy to use false evidence against him. Two witnesses accused Jesus of threatening to destroy the Temple. This could have been a distortion of the teaching recorded in

John 2:19 that when the Temple (his body) was destroyed it would rise again in three days.

At first Jesus did not reply to the accusation, but when he was put under oath and asked if he was the Messiah he replied: "So *you* say". Jesus did not agree with the High Priest but went on to explain his identity in his own terms (v64):

"You will see the Son of Man sitting on the right of the Almighty and coming on the clouds of heaven."

This was a reference to the book of Daniel (Daniel 7:13) which the members of the Sanhedrin would have been familiar with, and by saying this Jesus suggested that he was equal with God. This was as much as the High Priest needed to hear and in keeping with their laws he sentenced him to death:

"Anyone who blasphemes the name of the Lord must be put to death." Leviticus 24:16 (NIV)

The High Priest tore his clothes in outrage at the blasphemy and the others attacked Jesus, spitting, punching and mocking him.

Peter disowns Jesus

Matthew 26:69-75

During Jesus' trial before the Sanhedrin Peter was sitting outside in a courtyard. Several people approached him and suggested that they had seen him with Jesus, but three times he denied it, as Jesus had predicted. It was only when he heard a cock crowing that he remembered what Jesus had said, and he went away feeling deep regret at denying Jesus.

In the first three hundred years of the early church, Christians were severely persecuted and Matthew may have hoped that his readers would learn from Peter's mistake and not deny Jesus.

Activity

Write a short drama portraying Peter's denial of Christ. Try to express the feelings contained in the story.

Examples of early persecution of Christians

AD 64 – Nero covered Christians in tar and used them as candles for his garden parties.

Early 2nd century – Ignatius, Bishop of Antioch, was taken to Rome to be thrown to the lions.

Late 2nd century – Blandina, a slave girl from Gaul, was tortured and told to deny Christ but she refused:

"And after the scourging, after the wild beasts, after the frying -pan, she was at last thrown into a basket and presented to a bull." (New Eusebius 23)*

**A frying-pan was an iron chair which had a fire lit beneath it.*

Jesus is taken to Pilate

Matthew 27:1-2

Pilate, the Roman governor, was the only one who could officially sentence Jesus to death so the Jewish leaders handed him over for a second trial. The accusation that Jesus claimed to be the Messiah could easily be presented in a political nature – suggesting rebellion against the Roman Empire.

The death of Judas

Matthew 27:3-10

Judas had served the religious leaders' purpose and they no longer had any need for him. He soon realised that what he had done was wrong, but there was no turning back. He felt his situation was so hopeless that he returned the 30 pieces of silver and went out and hanged himself.

The money could not be put into the Temple treasury because it was blood money so it was used to buy a field which was used as a cemetery for foreigners. Matthew says this was a fulfilment of a prophecy in Jeremiah, but the exact prophecy is not contained there. It seems to be a combination of prophecies from Jeremiah 19: 1-13 and Zechariah 11:12-13 which Matthew must have quoted from memory inaccurately.

Suicide

Judas felt annoyed, guilty and angry with himself over what he had done, and he reckoned that there was no way out of his hopeless situation, so he took his own life. Sadly there are many people in our society who have done the same thing. In the UK and Ireland approximately 6300 people take their own lives every year, which is more than double the death toll from road traffic accidents.

Feelings of desperation, guilt, loneliness and hopelessness are all common human feelings but if they take control of a person's thinking they can have fatal results. The **Samaritans** is an organisation which provides emotional support to those who are despairing or feeling suicidal. Their trained volunteers provide assistance 24 hours a day mainly by telephone, but people are also able to drop in to their centres in person.

History of the Samaritans

The Samaritans

The Samaritans was founded by a London clergyman called **Chad Varah**. He was motivated to do something for those who were feeling suicidal after he had counselled some young people in despair and realised that what they needed was someone to listen to them – **befriending** is what he called it.

> *"I read in some digest that there were three suicides a day in Greater London. What were they supposed to do if they didn't want a Doctor or Social Worker from our splendid Welfare State? What sort of a someone might they want? Well, some had chosen me, because of my liberal views. If it was so easy to save lives, why didn't I do it all the time?"*

He set up a phone line and a drop-in centre for those in despair or feeling suicidal. Soon he was joined by helpers, whom he called Samaritans.

Rev Chad Varah

The work of the Samaritans is best summed up in two of their own Principles:

1. *The primary aim of the Samaritans is to be available at any hour of the day or night to befriend those passing through personal crises and in imminent danger of taking their own lives.*
2. *The Samaritans also seek to alleviate human misery, loneliness, despair and depression by listening to and befriending those who feel that they have no one else to turn to who would understand and accept them.*

Jesus before Pilate

Matthew 27:11-26

Jesus was brought before Pilate on a political charge: "Are you the King of the Jews?" Herod the Great had been called King of the Jews and if Jesus accepted the title for himself he was agreeing that he had political ambitions to govern Palestine and overthrow the Romans.

Jesus did not reply to anything Pilate said and gave him no reason to charge him. Pilate was frustrated at this and felt uneasy sentencing a man to death without any real evidence. He thought he might be able to free Jesus on the grounds that it was tradition to free a prisoner at Passover time. His troubled instinct about this case was confirmed by his wife who had been told in a dream not to have anything to do with Jesus. Pilate would have taken this seriously as everybody thought that Julius Caesar would not have been assassinated if he had taken his wife's dreams seriously. However, Pilate's idea was rejected by the crowd who preferred to have Barabbas, probably a Zealot, released instead. Pilate could only wash his hands to show that he did not agree, but he still did as the crowd wanted and sent Jesus to be crucified because he was aware that it was important to maintain good relations with the main religious leaders in Palestine and he did not want them to cause a riot.

Activity

Read the following statements from the Declaration of Human Rights. Look over the passages in this chapter again and try to identify all the ways in which Jesus was denied basic human rights.

Article 3.
Everyone has the right to life, liberty and security of person.

Article 5.
No one shall be subjected to torture or to cruel, inhuman or degrading treatment or punishment.

Article 10.
Everyone is entitled in full equality to a fair and public hearing by an independent and impartial tribunal, in the determination of his rights and obligations and of any criminal charge against him.

Article 18.
Everyone has the right to freedom of thought, conscience and religion; this right includes freedom to change his religion or belief, and freedom, either alone or in community with others and in public or private, to manifest his religion or belief in teaching, practice, worship and observance.

Questions

1 *a) Name the three disciples who were with Jesus while he prayed in the Garden of Gethsemane.*
b) Pick out three phrases from Matthew 26:36-46 which describe Jesus' sorrow.

2 *a) Why did Jesus not resist arrest in the garden?*
b) Where was Jesus taken when he was arrested?
c) What accusation was brought against Jesus about the Temple?
d) Of which crime did the High Priest find Jesus guilty?

3 *a) Try to think of situations today when Christians might be tempted to deny their faith?*
b) Why might Matthew have thought it a good idea to tell the story of Peter's denial of Christ to his readers in the early church?

4 *What part did Caiaphas play in the death of Jesus? Do you think he was to blame for the death of Jesus?*

5 *Imagine you are Pilate.Write down the reasons why you think you should let Jesus go and why you should crucify him.*

Amnesty International is an organisation which campaigns for human rights. It works on behalf of people who are arrested, imprisoned, tortured or killed for what they believe in. Try to find out more about this organisation. Some schools have an Amnesty International group and members write letters, or make petitions in order to bring about the fair treatment of prisoners or innocent victims.
To find out more about Amnesty International contact: 01232 666001

amnesty international uk

The Crucifixion, Death & Burial of Jesus

The soldiers mock Jesus

Matthew 27:27-31

The Roman soldiers took great pleasure in humiliating their prisoner who was supposedly the King of the Jews. They treated him in a cruel and demeaning way, spitting on him, hitting him and making him wear a scarlet robe and a crown of thorns as they bowed down to him.

Jesus is crucified

Matthew 27:32-44

It was usual to make a prisoner carry the cross-beam of the cross to the site of crucifixion. Jesus, however, had to have help, possibly because he was already so weak from the torturing and whipping. The soldiers forced Simon of Cyrene to carry the cross to **Golgotha** – the place of the skull.

The drink which Jesus was offered was a type of painkiller, but he refused it. He was crucified with two others and the reason for crucifixion was written at the top of each cross. The letters **INRI** appear in traditional pictures of the crucifixion. These are the four initial letters from the Latin translation of 'Jesus of Nazareth King of the Jews' – *Iesus Nazerenus Rex Iudaeorum.*

It is obvious that crucifixion was a public spectacle as Matthew records that people gathered to watch and even shouted abuse at those condemned. In the case of Jesus, the crowd laughed at his weakness and powerlessness and reminded him about his claims to have the power of God.

The death of Jesus

Matthew 27:45-56

During the last hours of Jesus' life, Matthew tells us that there were some strange and amazing events which occurred. Firstly, the whole region was covered in darkness, even though it was the middle of the day. Jesus was barely alive and called out *'Eli, Eli, lema sabacthani'* which meant 'My God, my God, why did you abandon me?' Some people thought he was calling for Elijah as it was believed by many that Elijah, who had never died, would make himself available to help those in need.

After Jesus had cried out and died there was an earthquake, people rose from the dead and the curtain hanging in the Holy of Holies was torn in two, from top to bottom. These events have clear symbolic significance. The torn curtain in the Temple shows the presence of God being freed from the Holy of Holies and being made available to all people. The dead being raised to life represented the future for all those who trusted in Christ's death as a sacrifice which would bring them forgiveness.

Jesus' death – a sacrifice for the world.

Christians believe that Jesus' death on the cross was no ordinary death. They explain the importance of his death by comparing it to a sacrifice. Jews sacrificed animals to God as a sign that they were sorry for their sins, and they received forgiveness in return. You could say that their sins were taken and put on the animal. In the same way Jesus was a sacrifice, only his death did not just take away the sins of a few people but the sins of the whole world. This means that Jesus was punished for all the things that people have done wrong so that they they could receive forgiveness from God. In summary, Jesus died:

- to save humans from the consequences of sin
- because no-one else was willing or able to pay the price for the sin of the whole world
- to restore humans to a right relationship with God.

Death by crucifixion

Crucifixion was one of several methods of capital punishment used during the time of Jesus, and it must have been one of the most cruel and humiliating. The Jewish historian Josephus described it as "the most wretched of deaths." Other methods included stoning, burning and beheading. Each method was associated with particular crimes; crucifixion, for example, was reserved for murder and rebellion.

A B C

According to historical sources it seems that thousands of individuals were killed by crucifixion. There is one report of a mass execution of 6000 followers of Spartacus as part of a victory celebration along the Appian Way in 71 BC.

The picture on the left (A) shows the traditional image of crucifixion – the victim is stretched upright and nailed by his hands and feet. Recently the accuracy of this has been questioned. In 1968 the bones of a man from the first century were discovered in a Jerusalem suburb called Giv'at ha–Mivtar. The skeleton had a nail through its right heel which suggests that the man died by crucifixion. Using the evidence, several theories have been formed about how a person was crucified and two of these are shown above (B and C). It is impossible to come to a definite conclusion on the basis of one piece of evidence and it would seem reasonable to conclude that there was more than one method of crucifixion.

Depending on the method used, death from crucifixion could last days or be as quick as a few hours. In most cases death would have resulted from suffocation, due to the inability to use the muscles needed for breathing.

After Jesus' death, Matthew says, the soldiers realised that he wasn't a mad man but "He really was the Son of God" (v54).

Activity

Look up the following references and see what New Testament writers thought of the significance of Christ's death:

Romans 5:6-11
Hebrews 9: 11-14, 28
1 Peter 3:18-19

The burial of Jesus

Matthew 27:57-66

Joseph of Arimathea was a wealthy man and, according to the Gospel of Mark, was a member of the Sanhedrin, so he must have been a secret friend of Jesus, and was putting himself at great risk by going to Pilate to ask for the body. He buried Jesus in his own tomb which was also a sign of his devotion. Normally corpses from crucifixions were burned at the town dump.

The tomb was sealed by a stone while the

two Marys sat and watched. A guard was placed by the tomb to make sure that the disciples did not steal the body and spread rumours of Jesus being resurrected.

Questions

1 a) What part did Simon of Cyrene play in the events leading up to the crucifixion?
b) Name the three groups of people who mocked Jesus on the cross.
c) Describe three of the supernatural events which happened when Jesus died.
d) What did the Roman soldier say after Jesus' death?
e) Why is the death of Jesus important for Christians today?

2 a) Who provided a tomb for Jesus' body and why was this significant?
b) Why was a guard placed at Jesus' tomb?

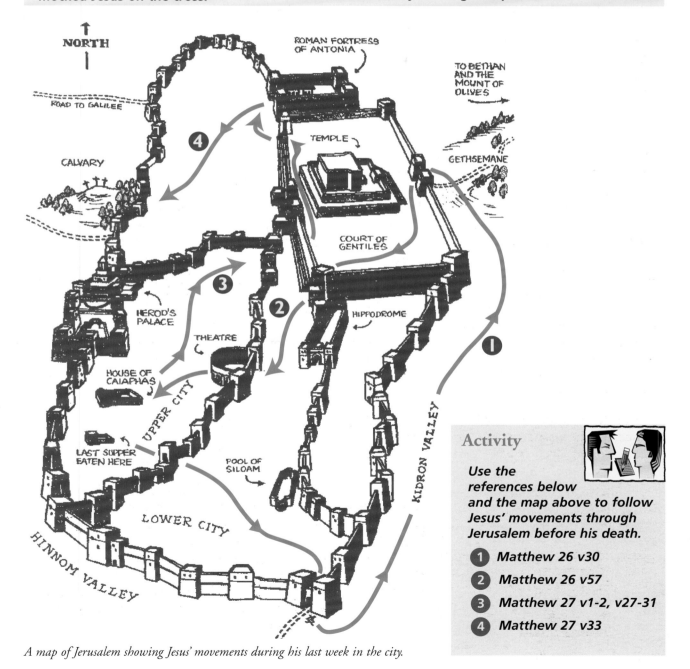

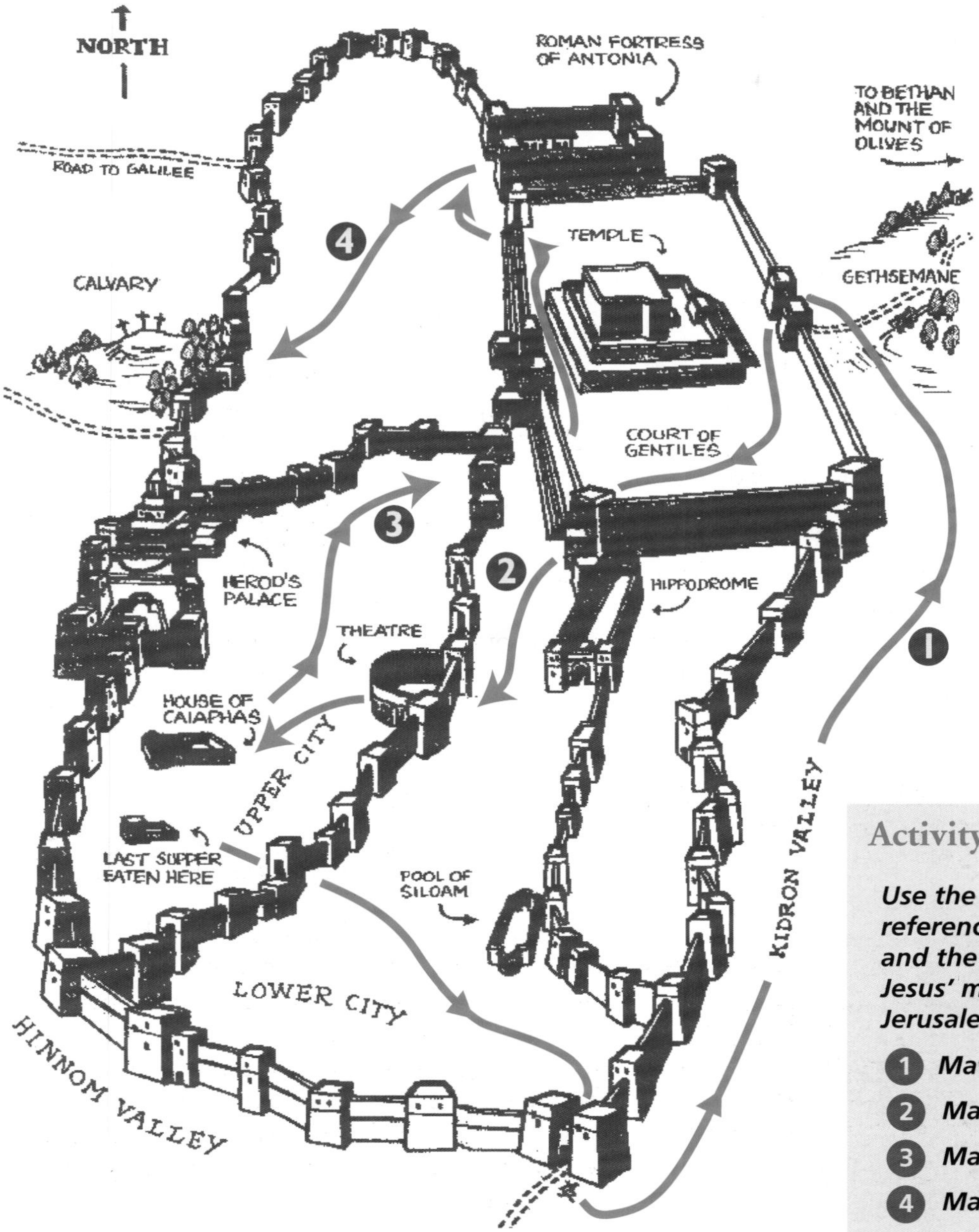

A map of Jerusalem showing Jesus' movements during his last week in the city.

Activity

Use the references below and the map above to follow Jesus' movements through Jerusalem before his death.

1. ***Matthew 26 v30***
2. ***Matthew 26 v57***
3. ***Matthew 27 v1-2, v27-31***
4. ***Matthew 27 v33***

The Resurrection Narrative

The Resurrection

Matthew 28:1-15

The two Marys, Mary Magdalene and the 'other' Mary who, Luke tells us, is Mary the mother of James, returned to the tomb on the Sunday morning. Again, there were more strange happenings – another earthquake, and an angel appeared and rolled away the stone from the entrance to the tomb. Matthew says that the soldiers were 'like dead men', which probably means they had either fainted from shock or were knocked out during the earthquake.

The angel then told his startling news to the two women – 'He is not here; he has been raised, just as he said.' To prove this he pointed to the empty slab inside the tomb where the body should have been. In an excited state, the women ran to tell the disciples what had happened, but before they got far they met Jesus and fell at his feet in worship. He instructed them to tell his disciples what had happened and said he would meet them in Galilee.

When the soldiers recovered from their shock they reported all the events to the Chief Priests who bribed them to say that the disciples had stolen the body.

The walk to Emmaus

Luke 24:13-35

In the gospels there are several examples of post-resurrection appearances recorded. In most cases Jesus appears or disappears in a supernatural way. It is clear that he is different from before and is not even recognised by some of his followers. This was the case when Jesus joined two men on the road to Emmaus. All we know about these men is that one was named Cleopas. When Jesus approached them he asked them what they had been talking about and they related to him all the events of the previous days – Jesus' trial and crucifixion and the story of the empty tomb.

Jesus scolded them for their lack of faith because they doubted that the one who had been crucified was the Messiah. They pointed out that he had not freed Israel from the Romans as the Messiah should have done. Jesus explained, however, that the Messiah was not a political figure as they had hoped and he used the Old Testament scriptures to back up his point that the Messiah was a suffering servant.

At the end of their journey the two men persuaded Jesus to eat with them, and it was only at the point when he ate the bread that they realised who he really was. Then Jesus disappeared and the men went straight back to Jerusalem and reported everything to the disciples who were discussing an earlier appearance of Christ to Simon.

Whatever people decide about the truth or fiction of the resurrection, Christians do agree that it proves several important facts:

1 Jesus is eternal and will come again.
2 Jesus was the Messiah.
3 There is life after death.
4 Jesus defeated the power of death and evil.

Discussion

Christians today are divided when it comes to understanding the resurrection. There are those who claim that it was a physical, actual event while others prefer to think of it as a spiritual resurrection described in picture-language in the Bible. Look at the following statements and decide which opinion is closest to your own:

"Jesus' death and resurrection were real events. The Bible does not lie. If it is a made-up story then the whole of the message of Christ's salvation is nonsense."

"The resurrection of Jesus was a spiritual event and the story which is associated with it is actually a type of picture-language describing the occasions when Christ's followers realised the meaning of his death and felt his presence with them."

"There are stories which grow up around the memory of every great leader or religious figure after they have died. The resurrection story is like a 'chinese whisper' which got out of control, but people are still foolish enough to believe it.'

"The message of the resurrection narrative is clear, even if the events are unclear – Jesus is alive today in heaven, and that's all that matters."

Activity

Organise a class debate on one of the following statements:
"Belief in the physical resurrection of Jesus is difficult in the 21st century"
"Without the resurrection the crucifixion has no meaning"

Questions

1. *What did the women see and experience when they went to Jesus' tomb on the Sunday morning?*
2. *a) Where did Jesus say he would meet his disciples after the resurrection?*
   b) What were the soldiers told to say about the empty tomb?
3. *a) Why did Jesus scold the men on the road to Emmaus?*
   b) How did they recognise Jesus?
4. *Explain why the resurrection is so important to Christians?*

Ascension, Commission & Promise to Return

Jesus appears to his disciples

Matthew 28:16-20

At this meeting with the disciples Jesus inspired them to carry on with the work he had started. This is called **The Great Commission** and Christians today believe that it still applies to them and that they too have a responsibility to spread the Gospel. Those who make it their life's work to share their Christian beliefs are called **missionaries**.

The Ascension

Acts 1:1-11

The book of the Acts of the Apostles is a continuation of the Gospel of Luke. In the first few verses it explains how the Gospel was an outline of Christ's life and the beginning of the Kingdom of God. The book of Acts is a sequel which traces the progress of the Kingdom of God in the early church.

Verses 6-11 explain that the disciples would receive help from the Holy Spirit but that Jesus must leave. This event is called the **Ascension** because Jesus did not end his life in death but was taken up into the sky and disappeared behind the clouds. Two men, probably angels, appeared and explained that although Christ had gone he would come back again in the same way.

Questions

1. *What reactions did the disciples have when they saw the risen Christ?*
2. *a) What is the Great Commission?*
   b) How do you think Christians might live out the Great Commission today?
3. *For how many days after his resurrection did Jesus appear to his disciples?*
4. *Describe Jesus ascension into heaven.*

Volunteer Missionary Movement
The Great Commission in Action

VMM is an ecumenical, lay Christian movement founded by Edwina Gately in 1969. It recruits volunteers in Britain and Ireland and sends them to churches and communities in Africa and South America. VMM missionaries believe that they should not only proclaim the Gospel to all people but that they should share their skills and talents to contribute to all aspects of human development: social, economic, political, psychological and spiritual.

Working together in a divided world

Here one volunteer, Barbara Hughes, tells her story.

What kind of Missionary work have you been involved in?

I was a volunteer for two years in an orphanage in Guatemala. My official rôle was Development Officer – fundraising, financial reporting and liaising with visiting groups. However, I fulfilled many other rôles especially journeying with the children in their emotional and spiritual development. I also provided educational help to children and the sisters and staff.

What inspired you to become a missionary?

I experience it very much as a vocation and a call to be in solidarity with the poor as Christ was. I was particularly inspired by the liberation theologians of Latin America who opened up for me a new way of living my Christian faith. Archbishop Oscar Romero would have been a very strong influence on my spiritual journey.

Do you think Christians today are obedient to the Great Commission?

Certainly the people I know are. I believe that those who are now practising Christians act from a conscious choice and are seriously looking for ways to make theirs a living faith.

How might people who are not missionaries try to live out the Great Commission in their lives?

I believe as Christians we are all missionaries. We have a mission to foster Christ's love in our own lives and to live in a manner which affords life and dignity to all. Therefore I believe we can live out our mission by living simply, aware of the affects our habits and actions have on others, by caring for ourselves, others and for the earth which the Lord has entrusted to us.

Answers page 15 Wordsquare

D	P	Z	D	K	Z	S	H	J	U	V	H	Z	X	C
S	T	O	L	A	E	Z	Q	F	G	P	T	F	J	D
B	Y	N	N	Y	C	S	R	G	G	D	U	A	H	E
C	I	N	S	T	Q	D	S	H	D	R	V	W	L	C
W	P	H	A	R	I	S	E	E	S	A	G	P	T	C
D	K	E	N	G	N	U	O	T	N	X	M	T	L	E
X	S	B	H	W	O	V	S	K	A	E	L	P	E	E
K	F	A	E	D	D	G	P	P	T	P	S	L	K	G
H	Y	I	D	E	D	M	U	N	I	G	I	X	U	Q
V	J	O	R	D	A	N	K	E	R	L	U	J	J	K
Z	D	Q	I	H	U	S	F	B	A	D	A	M	K	O
I	E	G	N	Y	U	C	B	G	M	T	O	T	C	A
F	W	W	F	L	D	M	E	L	A	S	U	R	E	J
F	F	H	M	M	P	A	L	E	S	T	I	N	E	N
C	X	P	S	N	L	T	K	V	S	R	B	D	J	H

Answers page 49 Crossword

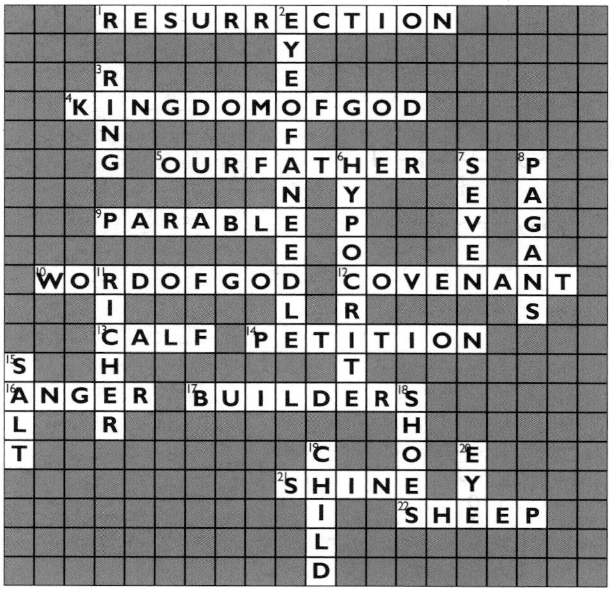

Answers page 62 Anagrams

miracles
foreigners
universalism
samaritan
zacchaeus
leprosy
religious leaders
allegory
pharisee
outcasts

Bible References

Chapter	Topics	References
1) Background to Palestine at the time of Jesus	i. Historical and geographical context	
	ii. Political background	
	iii. Social and religious context	
2) The Identity of Jesus	i. Birth	Mt 1:18-24, 2:1-23 Lk 1:26-56, 2:1-52
	ii. Baptism and Temptations	Mt 3:1-17, 4:1-11
	iii. Jesus' identity is questioned	Mt 8:23-27, 9:9-13, 13:53-58
	iv. Titles of Jesus	Mt 9:1-8, 9:27-34, 14:22-33, 15:21-28, 16:13-20
	v Transfiguration and Jesus in Jerusalem (I)	Mt 17:1-9, 21:1-17
3) The Teachings of Jesus	i. Discipleship	Mt 5:13-16, 7:24-29, 13:1-23, 18:15-20, Lk 14:25-33
	ii. Prayer	Mt 6:5-15
	iii. Forgiveness	Mt 18:21-35, Lk 15:11-32
	iv. Wealth and poverty	Mt 6:1-4, 19:16-30
	v. Humility and ambition	Mt 18:1-6
	vi. Life after death	Mt 22:23-33, 25:31-46
	vii. The new covenant	Mt 5:21-48, 26:17-30
4) The Deeds of Jesus	i. Religious leaders	Lk 14:1-24, 20:1-8
	ii. Women and the poor	Lk 4:38-40, 7:36-50, 8:40-56, 13:10-17, 21:1-4
	iii. Sinners	Lk 19:1-10
	iv. Social outcasts	Lk 5:12-14, 17:11-19, 18:35-43
	v. Foreigners	Lk 7:1-10, 10:25-37
5) Jesus' Death Resurrection and Ascension	i. Jesus in Jerusalem (II)	Mt 24:1-14, 26:17-35
	ii. Arrest and trials	Mt 26:36-75, 27:1-26
	iii The crucifixion, death and burial of Jesus	Mt 27:27-66
	iv. The resurrection narrative	Mt 28:1-15, Lk 24:13-35
	v. Ascension, commission and promise to return	Mt 28:16-20 Acts 1:1-11

Index